Improving Low Reading Ages
in the Secondary School

Most textbooks at secondary school have a reading age of twelve or more, whilst many struggling secondary school pupils have a reading age of nine or less.

What can a teacher do to bridge the gap?

This highly practical guide shows how learning support teachers and assistants can work effectively with secondary school pupils who are struggling with their reading. It relates to the direct working practices of teachers who work on reading recovery in secondary schools, steering them through issues such as:

- assessing the low-age reader;
- working with reading withdrawal groups;
- finding and creating resources for low-age readers;
- constructing spelling strategies to support reading;
- understanding the emotional dimension to being a poor reader;
- how to involve parents effectively.

The author offers valuable advice on how to make challenging mainstream subject textbooks accessible to low aged readers and help on where to find good free resources as well as commercial materials to suit them. Exploring the vital relationship between the mainstream and learning support function, he also outlines the ways in which the two can be harnessed to make a significant difference to reading improvement.

Special Educational Needs Co-ordinators, learning support teachers and assistants will welcome this much needed text, and will find it an invaluable resource in their aim to raise standards in both mainstream and small groups settings.

Paul Blum is currently a member of the Senior Management team at Islington Green School, North London.

Improving Low Reading Ages in the Secondary School

Practical strategies for learning support

Paul Blum

RoutledgeFalmer
Taylor & Francis Group

LONDON AND NEW YORK

£17-99

First published 2004 by RoutledgeFalmer
11 New Fetter Lane, London EC4P 4EE

Simultaneously published in the USA and Canada
by RoutledgeFalmer
29 West 35th Street, New York, NY 10001

RoutledgeFalmer is an imprint of the Taylor & Francis Group

© 2004 Paul Blum

Typeset in Baskerville by Keystroke, Jacaranda Lodge, Wolverhampton
Printed and bound in Great Britain by Bell & Bain Ltd, Glasgow

British Library Cataloguing in Publication Data
A catalogue record for this book is available from the British Library

Library of Congress Cataloging in Publication Data
Blum, Paul.
    Improving low reading ages in the secondary school: practical strategies
for learning support/Paul Blum.
        p. cm.
    Includes bibliographical references and index.
    ISBN 0–415–32909–4 (pbk.: alk. paper)
    1. Reading–Remedial teaching–Great Britain. 2. Reading (Secondary)–Great Britain.
    I. Title.
    LB1050.5.B57 2004
    428.4′071′2–dc22   2003018373

ISBN 0–415–32909–4

Contents

Acknowledgements

Page 38 from *Key Geography Foundations New Edition*, David Waugh and Tony Bushell (1996) is reproduced with the kind permission of Nelson Thornes Ltd.

Page 18 from *Discovering the Making of the UK*, Colin Shephard and Tim Lomas (1995) is reproduced with the kind permission of John Murray Publishers Ltd.

Material from *Buddhism*, Sue Penny (1995) is reprinted with the kind permission of Reed Publishers Oxford.

Introduction

Purpose and audience

This book sets out to advise learning support teachers who work with low-aged readers in secondary schools. But it will be a useful text to a wider audience of adults who work with the same group of pupils, such as: learning support assistants; parents who wish to support the improvement of their son's or daughter's reading at home; adults who work with pupils in lunchtime or after-school reading clubs; Special Needs Co-ordinators and local authority literacy consultants who train learning support staff to improve the reading of older pupils with low reading ages; secondary subject teachers who need to differentiate work in class for weak readers.

Overview

The book is divided into eight chapters that give practical advice and guidance on the following issues:

- how to assess a reading accurately using a range of commercial and home-made tests with particular emphasis placed on the emotional attitude towards learning
- how to work effectively with a reading group using a wide range of practical strategies
- how to encourage the reading of unfamiliar words using a mixture of phonic and non-phonic reinforcement strategies
- how to make the most of the relationship between learning support staff and subject teachers around in-class support situations involving reading
- how to seek out the best resources from the commercial publishers and the government
- how to differentiate work effectively in subject lessons and create materials that help weak readers gain access to the full secondary curriculum
- how to use spelling as a strategy to improve reading
- how to use Information Technology to improve both reading and writing.

Underpinning the information in this book is the good practice that learning support teachers and assistants have shared with me in training sessions and departmental meetings. The essence of the book is a pooling of practical tips that many secondary professionals have found useful in supporting pupils with their reading. There is a short glossary at the end of the book explaining technical terms relating to reading, and words in this glossary are highlighted in bold on their first occurrence in each chapter.

Setting the context for reading support

Learning support teachers play a pivotal role in providing reading support in secondary schools. They usually work with pupils who have been identified as having special educational needs, and much of the funding for their jobs comes into the school via the special needs budget. Special Education Needs pupils often have a multiplicity of learning, emotional and behaviour problems, but for many the underlying issue is that poor reading skills are making it hard for them to access the curriculum.

Low-aged readers: defining the challenges

Despite the rigorous attempts of the National Literacy Strategy to improve reading in primary schools, a significant number of children enter secondary school with reading ages well below their chronological norm. This has shown up statistically with the results at the end of Key Stage Two, where at least 17 per cent of pupils are failing to score National Curriculum level four in their reading. Many of these pupils continue to have reading ages between seven and ten when they are aged twelve to sixteen. It is not uncommon to find particularly high concentrations of low-aged readers in inner-city secondaries, with 50 per cent of Year 7 intakes reading at two years and more below their chronological age. Of this underachieving group the vast majority are boys.

There are new opportunities for reading recovery work offered by the extension of the National Literacy Strategy into secondary schools. The most important aspect of the National Literacy initiatives at Key Stage Three, in this regard, is the proposed structure for English lessons. This format suggests a twenty-minute slot in the middle of a lesson, where pupils divide up into groups, giving the class teacher, and any support teachers in the room, explicit time to work with readers at various levels. This process has been named 'Guided Reading'. The recommendation is that this time should be used to help low-aged readers to infer and deduce meaning from text. But this book demonstrates how this twenty minutes can go a lot further – creating a regular opportunity for a learning support teacher to help readers **decode** unfamiliar words in a text and work on improving their phonic skills, their store of **sight vocabulary** and their emotional attitude towards reading.

The emotional dimension

The majority of the pupils who work with learning support teachers at secondary school have already experienced many years of failure and frustration at their primaries. For pupils already burdened with negative emotions about their poor reading skills by the time they are eleven, the onset of teenage years is likely only to exacerbate these feeling of low self-esteem.

Such pupils find themselves in a secondary school system which is organized very differently from the primary system. The one class teacher is replaced with ten subject specialists, and the one classroom replaced with up to six room changes a day. This creates a major challenge to all pupils, let alone those who have pronounced reading difficulties. In this new fast-paced environment it's not surprising that struggling pupils can lose their motivation to improve their reading skills and instead devote their energies to hiding their problem.

Dyslexia and specific learning difficulty

Most of the low-aged readers in secondary school will have some kind of learning difficulty, often labelled *dyslexia*. Defining dyslexia always creates controversy amongst practitioners and researchers, and the focus of that debate is beyond the scope of this book. In simple terms, dyslexia can be defined literally as 'difficulty with words'. In practice, secondary school learning support staff will find themselves working with pupils who have significant literacy difficulties, the most common being problems with reading, writing and spelling. Some pupils can decode words but don't understand their meaning, and others can't decode but have good language awareness. Some read well but can't write or spell efficiently. It is common to find a combination of all these difficulties. Our target group of pupils will have fallen significantly behind their classmates and their lack of progress with the printed word will have become persistent and ingrained.

The role of a learning support teacher

There are a number of ways for learning support teachers to work with low-aged readers in this environment. Two specific routes usually present themselves:

- one-to-one or small-group work in the mainstream class
- one-to-one or small-group work through withdrawal from mainstream class.

The effectiveness of these methods of working depends on a number of institutional factors that vary from one secondary school to another:

- the school's overall ethos in learning support and literacy catch-up work
- the attitude of subject teachers to incorporating low-level readers into their lessons
- the skill and knowledge that the learning support teacher brings to assessing pupils with reading difficulty and then devising a programme of recovery work which will make a big difference to their reading competency.

We look in detail at these issues over the next eight chapters.

Chapter 1

Assessing the low-aged reader

Learning support teachers can work effectively with pupils only when they have a specific and detailed profile of their strengths and weaknesses as readers. This must include a look at their fluency for **decoding text** (mechanical reading of the words on the page), their level of understanding of what they read and their emotional attitude to the reading process itself. This information can come from a variety of sources:

- commercial reading tests
- home-made reading tests such as miscue analysis or phonological sound lists
- an emotional assessment of the pupil's attitude towards learning in general and reading in particular.

We will look at the pros and cons of each type of testing in this chapter and discuss how they can best be used in combination to gain detailed knowledge of the strengths and weaknesses of a struggling reader.

The profile of a good reader

The struggling reader needs to gain the skills that a good reader uses all the time. But what are these attributes? Good readers bring a number of skills together at the same time:

- the capacity to decode letter combinations they see and turn them into speech sounds
- the ability to access a whole store of remembered words and read them fluently, whenever they see them
- crucially, the talent to read words whilst simultaneously constructing meaning for them in their head.

Strong readers can also draw on a whole series of advanced skills to tackle difficult texts. They can build a meaningful narrative by making inferences and reading between the lines, sometimes re-reading sections they find hard or suspending judgement until the narrative progression of a passage is clearer. They bring their whole-life experience of language to make sense of the **context** they are reading about.

So what are the identifiable building blocks for this reading process? One of the simplest explanations, envisaging two pathways to effective reading, is usually called the dual route reading model. On the first pathway of the dual route, effective readers rely on **sight vocabulary** and are able to recognize, pronounce and know the meaning of a word at the instant of seeing it. This immediate whole-word recognition is called the **lexical** (whole-word) route to reading. But there are occasions when good readers cannot find a word in their instantaneous **sight vocabulary** because they don't remember it or have never seen it before.

In this situation the capable reader is forced to break a word down into its sounds. This type of text decoding is called the 'Sub-word' or **sub-lexical** route. It is the second pathway of the dual route. The reader first splits the word into its sounds (**segments** the word) and then rolls the sounds back together to create a word (**blends** the word).

Lexical and sub-lexical strategies are employed frequently when reading in the English language. Some words in English follow regular sound-to-letter mapping patterns. Examples of such regular words include 'bed', 'pump', 'brandy', 'hand', 'mistaken'. They can be read either by instantaneous whole-word recognition, the sight vocabulary of the lexical route or by breaking the word down into its constituent sounds, the strategy of the sub-lexical route. But irregular words such as 'sage', 'cough', 'island', 'garage', 'knock', 'meringue' and 'pint' cannot be decoded by segmenting words into their sounds (the sub-lexical route). They have to be memorized as sight vocabulary (the lexical route). Good readers can switch effortlessly and automatically from lexical to sub-lexical strategies for reading whenever they need to. But they also use **contextual** clues to help them predict what is happening in the narrative. Capable readers bring their linguistic and overall life experience to reading any passage. This helps them see where the narrative is going in terms of meaning and grammatical structure. For example, consider this short passage of writing.

She was told to look out for a row of red buses. In the middle of the row was the number 45.

The word 'row' can have two meanings, but here the context in which it is set implies that it is a line of buses rather than a noisy argument.

When you analyse the reading skills of low-aged readers you sometimes find that they have a poor memory for sight vocabulary and/or poor sub-lexical skills for breaking words down. Some are able to compensate for this by using context to help them work out unfamiliar words in the text, but many are poor at this as well.

As you carry out a variety of reading tests, they will reveal the lexical, sub-lexical and context prediction strengths of your weak readers.

The tests you try out on your readers can be a mixture of paid-for assessments and ones that you have made up yourself. The commercial tests are often a good starting point to give you an initial guide to your students' strengths and weaknesses, and you can explore these further in the home-made assessment you create.

Commercial reading tests

Commercial reading tests are the tests your school has to pay for. They are very carefully prepared to provide standardized information. They are piloted on a large sample of the population and take account of gender and socio-economic distribution. As a result of this sampling, the tests claim to be able to establish 'average age' capabilities for reading. They can be used at regular intervals and are a very useful way of measuring the progress of your low-aged reader, by giving you a base line score and then, through retesting, showing improvement over time. Each commercial test has strong selling points as well as individual limitations that we will discuss here. Information about where to get the materials can be found at the end of this chapter.

The Suffolk Reading Test

This test is published by NFER Nelson and is one of the most popular reading tests in British secondary schools. It is a group reading test: a learning support teacher can administer it to a group of pupils rather than to just one at a time. It is a multi-choice test that comes in several versions, so you can assess and reassess your pupils several times each year.

The Suffolk Reading Test has many good points. It's very quick to set and mark. The pupils complete it silently, making it a relatively natural way of testing their 'reading for meaning' skills. One limitation is that, since the test is multi-choice, there is always a one in five probability of scoring the right answer by guesswork alone.

The New Reading Analysis

The New Reading Analysis is also published by NFER and popular in secondary schools. It is an individual reading test, which the support teacher administers one to one. It is more complicated than the Suffolk Test, and training time for staff is much longer. But this investment in time gives a strong payback as it enables the teacher to pick up a truly detailed profile of the reader's strengths and weakness.

The New Reading Analysis has a series of six passages for the pupil to read, with comprehension questions. All the reading and questioning is done aloud.

Like the Suffolk Test, the New Reading Analysis has many good points. It allows you to spend some 'quality' time listening to your pupils as individual readers and assessing their skills. If you have a lot of knowledge of the reading process, this is an excellent chance to make some important observations of your pupil's personal strengths and weaknesses. This test gives you much more detailed information about the reading skills of your pupil than the general reading ages of the Suffolk Test. The results are broken down into both reading accuracy and reading comprehension. This is very useful, as pupils are often much better at one than the other. Knowing this is vital information in your assessment of them.

The personal approach of the New Reading Analysis make it a very good second and more thorough assessment after the initial Suffolk Reading Test. As you conduct it, there are a whole series of questions that you can look for answers to:

- Are pupils using phonological strategies when they get stuck (breaking down words into their sounds and then blending them back together again)?
- Are they panicking when they see long multisyllable words?
- What is their confidence level? How fluent are they?
- Do I get the feeling that they are holding the narrative development in their heads as they read?
- Are they prepared to misread a word or a sentence but plough on regardless?
- Do they try to give me an answer to a question about the text, without looking in the passage properly?
- Are they too nervous to look back at the passage and reread it on their own, while looking for an answer to a comprehension question?
- What is their body language and overall demeanour like as the reading aloud and comprehension take place?
- How often do pupils self-correct?

Home-made reading tests

Home-made tests are completely free of charge as they are tests that learning support teachers can make up themselves. They are non-standardized tests and so cannot give you an age-related result, but they can help you probe the specific weaknesses you suspect your readers have.

You can make up your own reading tests by selecting a short passage for your pupils to read or by putting together word lists. Here are some practical guidelines on setting up your own reading tests.

Selecting a text for a 'home-made' reading test

Research on reading improvement suggests that the comfort zone for reading effectively is 80 per cent accuracy. In this context, the reader is getting no more than two in ten words wrong. If the error rate is higher, the text is too hard; if there are many fewer errors than one in ten, the reader is well within the comfort zone.

In practice, it's almost impossible to pick a text which fits this rigid criteria. But if the pupil has chosen something they would like to read and it fits into this approximate level, then it makes sense to use it. If you pick a text for a miscue analysis, then it's a good idea to have two others ready, one harder and one easier. A text of between two and three hundred words is long enough.

Miscue analysis

When a pupil reads a short passage to you, you can examine the kind of mistakes they make and the strategies they try and use to self-correct. The notes that you make on the passage are called a miscue analysis, and can reveal useful patterns in reading behaviour. There are seven types of miscue:

word *Substitution.* The pupil puts another word in place of the correct one. Sometimes this is a non-word and at other times a real word that does or doesn't make sense in the context of the passage. Frequent substitutions are likely to put the pupil's comprehension under strain.

word *Refusal.* The pupil pauses on a word but does not attempt it. The teacher conducting the miscue analysis needs to work out a reason why the refusal has occurred. Did the pupil panic on a multisyllable word they did not recognize immediately? Did the pupil see a particular sound-to-letter pattern at the beginning or end of the word they do not feel comfortable with?

(word) *Omission.* The pupil leaves the word out. It is done quickly and appears to be an accident. Such omissions can make very little difference to the pupil's overall understanding of what they are reading, but they can be crucial. The teacher listening has to decide just how serious the missing word is.

|word *Insertion.* Adding a word that is not in the text. Like mistakes of omission, an additional word inserted can make very little difference to overall meaning or it can change the reader's comprehension significantly. If omissions and insertions happen frequently, the pupil is likely to lose overall understanding of the passage.

|word *Hesitation.* A pause of more than five seconds. Many hesitations are likely to indicate a loss of fluency and a struggle to hold meaning. Looking out for a pattern in the hesitations can be useful, as they may occur when certain phonological combinations are necessary to decode the text.

x2 word *Repetition.* The pupil repeats the word. Although this kind of mistake shows lack of confidence and fluency, it can reveal pupils' attitudes to working out things they find difficult. Repetition that reinforces the right word is interesting to monitor. Does the intonation improve on the second time of reading?

x2 word *Self-correction.* Tick a word if a self-correction occurs, and note how many repetitions it took to get the right answer. The way that self-correction occurs is one of the most interesting clues to reading patterns as it gives us strong clues as to pupils' strengths and weaknesses. Does the word get broken down into its sounds and said correctly? Is the word corrected after the pupil realizes the context it is in?

Using miscue analysis to assess specific reading skills

These are some of the checks that learning support teachers should make as they look for specific reading skills.

Fluency

- Is the pupil recognizing words immediately, without the need to sound them out?
- Is there some uncertainty and hesitancy in the reading?
- Is the pupil reading out one word at a time?
- Does the intonation of the pupil suggest confidence and engagement with the text?

Successful phonological processing

- When faced with an unfamiliar word, can the reader break down the word and sound it out?
- Do the miscues show that the reader can handle the initial letter sounds but no more?
- Do the miscues show that the reader can handle a wide range of sounds?
- Do the miscues show particular weaknesses with certain kinds of sounds and letter patterns?

Comprehension of meaning

You could check that pupils understand what they read by stopping them as they read. But it's probably less disruptive to conduct a full miscue analysis and let them read without interruption.

At the end, the interrogation for meaning could be done in the following ways:

- a short discussion about what has been read
- asking pupils to retell the story in their own words
- asking pupils to predict what will happen later in a story
- asking pupils to write about what they have read.

The problem with asking pupils to read aloud is they may concentrate so hard on reading accurately and fluently that they neglect the meaning of what they read. Instead, they focus on their practical performance and not their underlying understanding. When you ask them questions, it's useful to encourage them to look back into the text as a silent exercise.

Checklist around reading and body language

The way that pupils approach the process of reading can also provide some important contextual clues about their reading level:

- Do they ask for help all the time when they get stuck or do they never ask for help?
- Do they run a finger under the word they are reading?
- Are they showing any pleasure in reading or is it simply a chore?
- Are they fidgety and agitated while they read?
- Is there a lot of eye rubbing and yawning in the reading process?

Common problems reported by learning support teachers using miscue analysis

PROBLEM **?**

It's difficult to keep up with a reading pupil and mark down a passage with all the different types of miscue that we could observe.

SOLUTION ✓

Mark a text only for specific types of miscue and not for every possible type – for example substitution, insertion and omission rather than hesitation or refusal. Get the pupil to read the text into a tape recorder so you can listen to it as often as you want, later on. Keep the passage to a manageable length – two to three hundred words – so you don't fall behind them as they read.

PROBLEM **?**

Pupils put all their energy into reading aloud well at the expense of following the meaning of what they read: the performance, 'spotlight is on me', aspect of reading a text aloud.

SOLUTION ✓

Pupils read the text silently, on their own, so they get the feel for the meaning of it before reading it aloud. Then they describe what they've read aloud. They retell the story. They read

continued

the text aloud, stopping every two minutes to discuss the details of what they are reading in more detail with you as they go along.

PROBLEM **?**

The passage being used for the miscue analysis isn't right. The pupil is finding it too difficult or too easy.

SOLUTION ✓

Remember that 90 per cent or more accuracy indicates that the passage is probably too easy; 80 per cent is probably a sufficient challenge to be a useful learning experience. Below 80 per cent, accuracy is too challenging. Try to have a couple of other passages of varying levels available, so you can change the text if you have to.

A readability test

The Basic Skills Agency has devised a simple test to work out approximate reading age. This is supplied on a small card, which can easily slip into a planner or wallet. The test is very simple but it's a quick way of measuring a reading age and you can use it to find texts that are at different levels of difficulty for a miscue analysis. It's also a quick way of working out how difficult the reading material is in class. If you are doing in-class support, you can help the mainstream teacher by doing a quick assessment of the reading materials they are using. The readability test is called the Smog Reading Reckoner and is available free of charge from the Basic Skills Agency on a handout called 'Making Reading Easier'.

Phonological skills

All explanations of how young children learn to read stress the importance of seeing certain letters and letter combinations and being able to break them down into appropriate sounds. But the majority of low-aged readers at secondary school find it a struggle to improve their mechanical reading of text, using sounding out. In this case they have faulty phonological skills.

Standardized commercial tests such as the New Reading Analysis can expose this as a general problem but you may wish to find out more specific details about the sound/letter combinations your pupil is finding hard. Here are some examples of made-up assessments that can help you do this. They are easy to put together on the spot in a reading lesson but you can get plenty of ideas from the lists in practical textbooks such as Reason and Boote's *Helping Children with Reading and Spelling*.

Home-made phonological tests

As a useful starting point in creating home-made assessment, consider asking your pupils to write out the letters A to Z and sound them out to you. Next you could offer a basic check list of the common letter combinations pupils are likely to see in English. See how many of them they can read. A sensible starting point for these kinds of lists would be the common letter combinations at the beginning of words.

ch sh th wh qu bl br sc sk sl sn sp st sw tr tw cl cr dr dw fl fr gl gr sw ph wr pl pr

Then move on to triple letter combinations at the beginning of words:

scr shr sph spl spr squ str thr

After the examination of how your pupil manages with the beginning of words, you could look at their phonological skills with common word endings:

-ft -mp -air -ild -igh -ie -ay -are -ow -oy -ue -ble -dle -gle -kle -ple -tle -dge -tch -sion -tion -ed -er -mb -nch -nd -ng -nk -nt -ore -ould -ic -ing -ly -ment -ness

There follow examples of short tests I have made up. But you can really do anything you want to customize the test to the pupil.

The first is an initial blends test – illustrated with some words and some non-words:

bl

blor	black
blob	blorp
blon	block
blot	blush
blap	

The same kind of test could be made up for other initial combinations such as *br, dr, fl, pl, sl, sw, tr* and *tw*.

Here is a small test I made up to assess a pupil's ability to process short vowel sounds:

a	*e*	*i*	*o*	*u*
at	hen	is	on	up
bat	pen	his	pot	cut
cat	red	pit	hot	fun
fat	fed	sit	dog	gun
mad	beg	lit	fog	jug
jam	peg	wig	box	rug
map	net	pig	fox	sun
bag	pet	pip	dot	
tap	yet	zip		

The next home-made test relies on your pupils being able to work out the first part of the word. It is a short assessment of common word endings in a mixture of words and non-words.

ng

bling	wong
sing	long
ring	sailing
thing	perling

lt

belt	kilt
melt	felt
swelt	silt
shelt	wilt

Spoonerisms

Testing your pupils with some spoonerisms is another effective way of seeing how confident they are at **blending** and **segmenting** letter sounds. You should explain to the pupil that you are going to ask them to play around with word sounds. Here is an example:

If I say: **c**ar **p**ark	You say: **p**ar **c**ark
If I say: **J**ohn **L**ennon	You say: **L**on **J**ennon

Now continue with some famous names. You are likely to find that a pupil with poor phonological skills finds spoonerisms very difficult.

For some pupils who rely on visual clues, it will be important not only to say the spoonerisms but also to write them down, so the pupil can write the letter reversal at the beginning of the word and then read it back to you.

Multisyllable non-words

This is a quick non-word test to assess how well your pupil can remember the sounds at the beginning of the word by the time they get to the end of saying them aloud. It measures blending and sound memory skills. The non-words here are only an example and you can easily make up your own list to suit the sounds you want to test.

roborptwell	latoprelsin
lisolrip	mipolusturp

Making an emotional assessment

One simple quotation sums up the importance of this section. It was penned by an experienced reading teacher to a mainstream teacher who had asked for advice on how to help a Year 8 pupil. With the full force of forty years' specialization in this field Ann Leslie wrote: 'Whatever you do, it's important not to create a sense of anxiety. Confidence, as you know, in reading and writing is eventually the most important factor.'

The emotional dimension to the problems that low-aged readers experience at secondary school is almost always underestimated. Yet it is probably the main issue in helping pupils improve their reading. If you are working with a pupil in any one-to-one or small-group situation, you need to find out just how they feel about the process of learning in general and reading in particular.

Research on early learning experiences has shown that dealing with new situations is always a potentially fraught experience. Yet those who have been successful in repeated learning experiences get used to the feeling of stepping into the unknown. They overcome the anxiety that each new learning situation brings. But some learners fail to conquer a new learning situation. They are overstretched by it and instead learn feelings of stress and failure. If this happens more than a few times, they also start to learn defensive measures to avoid those situations. All learning is about taking a risk, the risk that you might fail and fall flat on your face. Those who regularly fail in their early experiences of a particular activity are going to want to avoid taking such risks.

This certainly accounts for the way poor readers at secondary school often opt out of further self-improvement, having had at primary school years of feeling insecure about their abilities.

Some of the teachers whom these low-aged readers encounter will be insensitive to their feeling of failure. It will not have been their own personal experience of being at school. School was a place in which they were successful. It was an institution that they have decided to return to, for an adult working life. Such teachers will be very impatient with the defensive strategies they see their poor readers using and will readily label them as negative behaviours. Time and time again teachers will describe off-task behaviour and low concentration levels as a pupil being lazy, naughty or giving up too easily. These teachers will allow these negative feelings to rule their professional commitments to poor readers. Even the vast majority of well-intentioned teachers who fight hard to remain sensitive to the feelings of frustration and poor self-esteem that their low-aged secondary readers have will find it difficult always to empathize positively. Research on the emotions of learning highlight how frustrated and disgruntled learners often transfer their negative feelings on to their teachers.

Emotional impact

For poor readers, who are scoring only low level 3 or level 2 in their English SAT at the age of ten, reading is likely to be an unpleasant activity, whereas for most of their teachers, being highly literate, the opposite is true.

Whilst all struggling reader have their own sets of individual problems that are very personal to their reading histories, there are general patterns of development that are worth considering. The following description is a stereotype which many of our weak readers will have experienced in part or whole.

Most disaffected low-aged readers are likely to have problems with breaking unfamiliar words down into letter sounds. For them reading has become very much a school activity only. When younger they didn't visit libraries or have lots of books and other types of texts in their homes, and the main source of story telling and narrative was watching the television or a video. They got progressively more alienated with reading as the school texts started to get more varied and difficult. As the language of the reading got more abstract and difficult, they found it more and more of a tiresome chore. Such pupils became more aware that they were falling behind their classmates and started to cut off from the reading experience, whenever they could.

Unfortunately, the common approach of secondary schools to practising reading didn't rekindle their interest and did little to help them. Most schools tend to create general reading time in English lessons or in form-tutor periods in which pupils read quietly to themselves.

Whole-class silent reading

Sessions of whole-class silent reading sometimes take place in the school library, sometimes in the classroom. Pupils are expected to read their books in silence. All too often, the good readers sink themselves into their text. But many of the class pick up a different text every week and fidget and fiddle with it, rather than read it. They try to get up to change it many times, often spending most of the reading lesson looking for another book. While the sophisticated readers become engrossed in their text, many of the inadequate readers start to smirk behind the books, using the covers to hide talking and whispering.

Pupils who fall into our reading recovery category often look at their book but fail to engage. They find a forty-five minute slot of silent reading a very negative emotional experience, which reaffirms their sense of personal failure with reading.

This leaves a learning support teacher with much to do to win back interest and enthusiasm for the process or reading. Working with the emotional side of these pupils in and out of class is one of their most important jobs.

Auditing the low-aged reader's emotional state

Each individual has a different emotional response to having poor reading skills and being behind the rest of the class. Here are some simple things to check out:

- Watch your pupils in as many different lessons as possible. In which parts of the curriculum do they seem confident? What good teaching strategies do you see being used there? Is the pupil allowed to use a range of learning styles in these lessons?
- Ask your pupils which lessons they are happiest and most confident in. You'll learn a lot from their answer.
- Talk to a range of subject teachers about the emotional approach your pupils have to learning. This will add a further dimension to your knowledge.
- Work out how your pupils get round the problem of lots of difficult reading material in any given lesson. Are they getting verbal explanations of what's in the text from another pupil or the teacher? Are they simply switching off to the lesson and misbehaving? How do some teachers reverse this negative slide into low levels of motivation?

Further reading

Theory of reading

Funnel, E. and Stuart, M. (eds) (1995) *Learning to Read: The Psychology of the Classroom* (Blackwells). Interesting chapters by different authors on the reading process. Chapter 2 by Morag Stuart is very pertinent on the dual route model.

Bielby, N. (1994) *Making Sense of Phonics: New Phonics and its Practical Implications* (Scholastic). This describes the importance of context and prediction in the reading process in much more detail. But it also examines the importance of meaning, orthographics, phonology and context in lucid detail with some useful practical examples.

Adams, M. J. (1990) *Beginning to Read: Thinking and Learning About Print* (Cambridge, MA: MIT Press). Like Morag Stuart, Adams emphasizes the importance of sound-to-letter mapping skills in the reading process. But it has many interesting reading strategies to suggest.

Reason, R. and Boote, R. (1994) *Helping Children with Reading and Spelling: A Special Needs Manual* (Routledge/Falmer). This is a classic text on literacy recovery. Although geared to primary school pupils, it is full of useful wisdom and advice that can be applied to the secondary setting. You can read more about the practical factors that influence reading ability in this book.

Commercial reading tests

Hagley, F. J. (1986) *Suffolk Reading Test* (NFER–Nelson).

Vincent, D. and De la Mare, M. (1985) *New Reading Analysis* (NFER–Nelson).

It may be useful for you to read the full details about how the tests were put together. Most schools buy the teacher manual that accompanies each test.

Emotional assessment

Dean, Geoff (2000) *Teaching Reading in Secondary Schools* (Fulton). Dean's book bravely debunks the reading improvement process that goes on in many secondary schools. The book shows how secondary schools can fail to teach higher level literacy skills.

Creating home-made reading tests

Mcguiness, C. and Mcguiness, G. (1998) *Reading Reflex: The Foolproof Phono-graphix Method for Teaching Your Child to Read* (Penguin). This has some useful word tables based on key sound patterns, which you could dip in and out of to help you make your own word lists. The book's useful materials for over-elevens are limited by 'infant' illustrations.

Reason, R. and Boote, R. (1994) *Helping Children with Reading and Spelling: A Special Needs Manual* (Routledge/Falmer). As well as being useful on reading theory, this book has excellent word lists based around certain sound-to-letter mappings. An excellent source of ideas for your own word tests.

Chapter 2

Working with reading withdrawal groups

The National Literacy Strategy encourages group work on reading as a part of a guided reading session in the middle part of a lesson. Some schools have responded directly to this and keep their struggling readers in the classroom to do this work with a learning support teacher or an assistant. But the majority of secondary schools still operate the system of 'withdrawing' small groups of weak readers from the class. Most learning support teachers will experience reading withdrawal groups as an 'out of mainstream' phenomenon.

How to make a reading withdrawal group work well

Generally speaking it's important to remember that pupils with low reading ages respond better to being taken out of their classrooms for structured reading sessions when they are in Years 7 and 8. As they move up the school they are more inclined to see withdrawal from their lessons as negative attention. Your best chance of making a difference to their reading age comes when they are fresh to the school. My experience of working with these groups indicates that reading scores rise most sharply in the first two terms of Year 7.

Out-of-class withdrawal work

It's probably easiest to have a positive emotional impact in this environment. The pupils will be seeing their learning support teacher on their own or in a small group. They are away from the mainstream class situation where their teacher has a wide range of abilities to cater for and finds it hard to give them proper one-to-one attention. In this situation the Learning support teachers have the chance to build their own positive emotional learning environment without having to worry about the rest of the class and what the mainstream teacher is doing to manage it. A reading withdrawal group is likely to work well if you take note of the following points in preparing to teach your reading group.

Ten steps to ensure an effective group reading

- Make sure that you have prepared a session that is based on an accurate assessment of each pupil's strengths and weaknesses – the kinds of observation that we looked at in detail in the last chapter. Build on a pupil's prior knowledge, interests and enthusiasms. Always make this your starting point as it will help breathe life into reading recovery work every single lesson.
- Take every opportunity you can to boost the confidence of the pupils in your group. Making them feel positive about themselves is a prerequisite for everything you do. Work out reward systems carefully and use lots of praise. We will explore this in more detail later in this chapter.
- Try to create a sense of fun in the work around reading that you do. This enjoyment and engagement should lead to a sense of momentum and pace.
- Teach in a small step-by-step approach, so it's almost impossible for the pupils to feel unsure of what's going on. This is sometimes described as creating an 'error-free' environment.

- Find good texts – both fiction and non-fiction texts that enthuse your pupils. This is sometimes described as offering 'real reading' opportunities. Without a narrative that holds pupils' interests, a reading withdrawal group is never going to gain its own momentum. We will look at the materials available for teenagers with low reading ages in Chapter 5. At this stage it is worth pointing that there are far fewer good texts for secondary-aged than for primary-aged pupils.
- Build up your pupils' phonic skills. Most secondary students with literacy problems have sound-to-letter mapping inadequacies. The work you do on phonological processing will be essential, but deciding on how to do it effectively is just as vital. A light touch with imagination and invention is necessary, or you will destroy the sense of fun and feelings of confidence so vital to a successful reading intervention.
- Use a mixed bag of interventions, whenever possible. Prioritizing phonological skills may be important to improving the way your pupil reads, but reading can also be improved with other reinforcement activities such as speaking or writing about the text and building a store of sight vocabulary.
- Always use a strategy called **over-learning**. Your pupils have low levels of confidence from their frequent past failure to learn. They need a lot more repetition and reinforcement than other students. When you are reading with them, try to give those opportunities to them.
- Involve parents. This is one of the hardest areas of work at secondary school, but vital if the work of the reading withdrawal is to be reinforced by further work in the home. (We will look at specific ways of encouraging parents later in this chapter.)
- If you have set your readers personal targets for their group sessions, then you will need to remind them of what the targets are at the start of every session. For example, before a pupil reads, you point out that you want to see them using the strategy of breaking unfamiliar words into their sounds and then **blending** together again.

In a reading withdrawal group that is working well, learning support teachers can measure their own success in terms of improvements in the following skills in their pupils:

- Pupils can talk about the text they are reading.
- They can predict how the narrative will develop.
- They can retell the story, describing characters and character interchange in the text.
- They can use specific language from the text.
- They show by the way that they read aloud that they can scan ahead, reread and self-correct.
- They can distinguish between fiction and non-fiction. Also between genres of writing such as reports, instructions, stories and poetry.
- They can make inferences about the motivation and attitude of the characters.
- Their self-confidence is increasing and this is shown by an greater fluency in their reading.

Practical strategies for working with reading withdrawal groups

Before the reading starts

There are a number of ways of interrogating texts that can involve pupils in pre-reading tasks. The most important preparation is to give the pupil a book with a suitable reading level. One or two mistakes in every ten words represent a zone of comfort but not much more. Other useful pre-reading activities include:

- reading the title on the front cover with the pupils
- getting the pupils to find the name of author or illustrator, and maybe publisher and ISBN
- asking the young people to scan through the book to look for clues about the names of the main characters

- if there are pictures, getting pupils to predict what they think the story will be about
- before starting a reading session, asking the children to find 'important words' or 'difficult words': practise reading them and work out what they mean
- helping pupils decide on the genre of their text. Is it fiction or non-fiction? Is it crime or mystery? Is it sci-fi or romance? Once the pupils have decided on a genre, see whether you can get them to tell you what they expect the likely conventions of that sort of writing to be.
- Mixing up the strategies above, sometimes doing them *all* as a pre-reading task, other times only doing one or two.

During reading aloud

While pupils read aloud they should be encouraged to try different strategies when they get stuck. This is often best done by getting them to question themselves about the text. Here are some good examples.

- What word would make sense here?
- Does the sentence I have read sound right?
- Is there a picture I can use to guess this word?
- Does the word look like another one that I know? If so, how would it sound?
- Did I get the right sound at the beginning of the word?
- Can I say the last part of the word correctly?
- Shall I break the word down into its sounds and then roll it back together?

Self-help strategies

You could experiment with one or all of these strategies that pupils can use when they get stuck on an unfamiliar word. Encourage them to:

- reread a word, phrase or sentence
- listen to themselves read – to see if it is making sense
- move a finger along the lines so they know exactly which word they are on
- use pictures to help them follow the narrative
- look for words within words to help them when they are stuck ('chunking'). Examples: e*clip*se, marri*age* – both these longer words have smaller and more manageable words within them
- look ahead for words which they can recognize
- break a word down into its letter sounds: 'mis/un/der/st/and/ing'. This is called **segmenting**. One useful technique is to encourage the pupil to say a word aloud in a robot's voice. Then roll it together again (Blending).

Teachers can reinforce this activity by testing pupils. After covering the word with your finger, you can ask them to say the first part of the word, the second part, the last part, all the word or some of the word. You can change the order in which pupils do it. This exercise helps pupils to practise the letter sounds. For more detail on this technique see Chapter 3, p. 30.

Another useful strategy to teach the pupil is to miss out the difficult word and read ahead to the next comma or full stop. This may help the pupil to pick up hints which will identify the earlier unknown word.

Praise, patience and prompting

Praise

Here is an interesting little experiment for you to carry out which demonstrates the importance of praise. Read a passage with a pupil, half of it with no verbal response from you, either praise or criticism, and half of it punctuated with a lot of verbal praise. You are likely to find that positive momentum built from just high levels of general praise, buoys up your reader and that he or she starts making fewer mistakes. In a reading test where the teacher sits stony-faced, doesn't make eye-contact and doesn't praise or encourage, the child's performance dips. In a reading test where some praise is given, the child's performance is significantly higher. All this is unscientific analysis, but it points strongly to the emotional and psychological bond between reader and adult being hugely important. General praise and rewards create a good psychological atmosphere for reading aloud to take place.

Praise linked to rewards

Praise that links in with a merit system is always useful. Low-level, high-frequency rewards encourage engagement with the lesson. This is an additional incentive on top of verbal encouragement. Any system of reward implemented regularly, at home as well as at school, is likely to lead to more reading practice taking place.

When working with a small group or one-to-one, there are a lot of strategies that become easier to operate because of the low pupil-to-teacher ratio. Here is a suggested framework for positive reinforcement with small groups.

The positive reward stamp

Using a positive reward such as a stamp inked with 'very good' or a 'smiley face' is an excellent strategy for a whole class of thirty. But it's even better in a withdrawal group because it's much easier to administer to a group of fewer than eight. As we saw earlier in this chapter, the literacy-recovery pupils respond to learning experiences which are built on small regular steps that are easy to succeed at (the 'errorless learning environment'). Within this framework, they respond to regular positive affirmations of their success.

The reward stamp, given out three times in a forty-five minute lesson, creates this important intervention climate of step by step positive momentum. This kind of reward is a low-level, high-frequency inducement: low-level in that a pupil can get it for a range of little things; high frequency in that a pupil is awarded it three times in one lesson.

Giving out three rewards a lesson could get a pupil twelve in only four lessons. You could link each ten in with another form of school reward such as a merit slip, certificate or house point. The low-level reward gives students with a poor opinion of themselves a chance for a regular positive token. It bolsters the emotional climate around them.

You can give the students a simple grid of fifty squares and get them to stick it in their diaries, planners or exercise books. Each stamp goes into one of the squares. As ten are converted to another official form of school reward, you can sign over the last one in the series. An alternative is to get them to draw a grid into their books and number them.

Reward stamps can be used for a mixture of positive attitudes and efforts with reading withdrawal groups. These are some of the most likely:

- good 'on-task' behaviour during the lesson
- meeting specific learning objectives for that lesson, in relation to speaking, reading or writing. In small-group situations you can remind individual students of their specific reading targets. (A list of likely targets follows later in this chapter.)
- acts of collaboration that involve supporting another pupil in the withdrawal group – for example, prompting them when they read aloud
- demonstrating some aspect of the learning to the whole group (maybe writing on the white board or overhead, or reading out a piece of their work).

There may be a specific behaviour or concentration target that you negotiate with certain pupils. In some cases, the receiving of a specified number of reward stamps could link to a praise letter or phone call home. I've used this with a pupil with very disruptive behaviour. The reward stamps were linked to five-minute slots of not talking to anybody and writing at least five lines.

What you decide to link the reward stamp to is up to you. It gives the opportunity to reward students every fifteen minutes of a lesson and helps build the momentum for learning. Anticipating when the reward stamps will be given out is a ritual that keeps the students entertained. As a routine, it helps to keep the teacher focused on what students are doing which is positive, even during turbulent parts of the lesson. Of course, the reward stamp is not an end in itself. Regular words of praise and encouragement will sustain the learning experience every minute of a lesson and not just three times in forty-five minutes.

Here are some reasons for using the low-level reward stamp:

- It's quick and easy to use.
- It's a positive stroke, given regularly in the lesson.
- It keeps you and the pupils focused on what is going right rather than on problems. In any difficult lesson when many pupils are challenging your authority, it is a strategy that keeps you from being pulled down into totally negative interactions.
- It helps to build on the reading recovery intervention philosophy of small steps towards larger goals, in an environment in which getting something right becomes a much more likely outcome than getting it wrong.
- Collecting the stamps entertains the pupils. It's not just entertainment for Year 7s. If you take it seriously, the older ones will take it seriously as well.
- It's easy to tie your low-level, high-frequency reward system into more formal systems of merit, run by the school, so that your students' good work in reading sessions get recognized elsewhere.
- It also links in well with reward systems that you can establish with the parents of 'low-aged' readers, through communications home.

Specific praise

Your praise can be linked to the individual targets that you have set with the pupils – targets linked to specific improvements in their reading that you have told them you are looking out for:

- thinking about what they are reading
- noticing letter sounds
- stopping if they make a mistake, rather than ploughing on
- trying to work words out without asking you every time they are stuck
- rereading a phrase to try to get it right
- looking for a pattern they know in an unfamiliar word
- using the pictures to help them
- for pupils with low concentration span, praise for staying on-task for a specific amount of time.

It's important to praise both for a successful and for an unsuccessful attempt. The pupils need to know that they are using the right strategy even when they get it wrong. Practising a strategy can be more important than getting the right answer.

Patience during the reading process

We have dealt with all the ways in which you can go about prompting the reader. But one key strategy is to let the reader have time to select a way forward for themselves.

Avoid the spoon-feeding syndrome. Don't necessarily give the pupil the word, every time they get stuck. Watch out for classmates who try to prompt them, even when you're not doing so. Stop them whispering the answer, making the first sound in the word or even moving their lips in a certain way to provide help.

Give the pupil time. For example a pupil may be trying to think of a strategy to work out a difficult word. He is scanning a picture and trying to reread the sentence when you butt in by trying to get him to sound out the word. He does as you ask and the potentially successful strategy he was going to use will be wiped out of his mind. This will undermine confidence and independence. Make sure that you remain silent yourself if you want to give pupils the chance to develop their own strategy.

Prompts

On the other hand, there are times when prompting is sensible – especially when you need to move the narrative along briskly, to establish pace and momentum so that all pupils stay engaged with the story line. You may want to provide key words to a pupil quickly so that the story keeps moving.

We have looked at self-help strategies that pupils can be encouraged to adopt in order to help them with their reading. What makes a good prompt? Good prompts

- give just enough help to get the reading moving again
- are short but still remind pupils of the self-help strategies they use in their reading (for example, sounding out a word or checking for meaning). These could be cued in with a simple phrase such as 'Sound it out' or 'Is it making sense?'
- remind the pupils that there is more than one way to sort out the problem they are having. A good phrase is: 'Why don't you try a different way?'

Some examples of good prompts:

- Does it look like a word you know already?
- Think about the meaning of the sentence.
- Look carefully at the first few letters in the word.
- Think of a word that makes sense and sounds right.
- Use that picture to help.
- Reread the sentence.
- Leave out the hard word and read on, then go back and try it again.
- Break a long word up into smaller bits.
- Can you see a pattern of letters that you know in the word?
- Read everything on the left of my finger.
- Now on the right.
- Can you roll the two bits of the word together?

The 'Spotlight is on me' phenomenon

If you work with any group of pupils in reading withdrawal groups, you may have noticed an interesting phenomenon. Individual pupils are able to give the right answer to a reading problem when it's not their turn to read aloud. They can prompt another pupil effortlessly yet are frozen to the spot when it's their turn to read to the group. With the spotlight on them, they feel ashamed and stressed.

Reduction strategies

Allow one pupil to help the reader, by prompting them when they get stuck. You may agree to let this happen after ten seconds of waiting have passed.

Experiment with paired reading: ask two pupils to take it in turns to read to each other. This strategy helps to reduce the spotlight effect and highlights the fact that one pupil can be a great teacher of another – especially if it is somebody the first pupil trusts and knows has similar reading difficulties. Often, a pupil looking over a shoulder of a reader can read the difficult words and take away the tensions of reading aloud.

Try some 'quick-fire reading'. One pupil reads a sentence or a paragraph before you pass the reading on to somebody else, sometimes in order around the table, other times at random. This keeps pupils focused, as they are never far from their turn and their turn is never long before the 'spotlight' moves on.

Try choric reading – reading together with the teacher. The group recites the lines in unison. This gives a weaker pupil the sense of fluency without having to get every word correct.

Try voluntary reading nomination: pupils pick the next person to read after them. The selected person can read as little or as much as they want before themselves selecting another member of the group. This process creates an atmosphere of unpredictability and entertainment. The spotlight doesn't have to stay on an individual for too long.

Read to the pupils in your group so that they get a good feel of what the passage is about and the words they will encounter. Keep the passage relatively short. Then get your strongest reader to read the same passage again. Pass the same piece of reading around the group so that the weaker readers will have already heard it several times before they attempt to read it themselves 'under the spotlight'.

Try to find short plays to read with them. Plays naturally give out parts to the readers and the pupils often enjoy taking their turn within this kind of structure.

Always variety

In your role as the teacher/group facilitator it is worth remembering always the phrase 'variety is the spice of life'. So mix up the strategies you use to get the group to share the reading:

- sometimes stopping to question the meaning of the text, sometimes stopping to prompt a pupil through a problem, but at other times allowing fluency at all costs, even when mistakes have been made
- sometimes quizzing individual pupils on an area of learning that they are supposed to be improving on
- other times asking for general opinions from any volunteer in the group.

This variety will keep pupils on their toes and involved in the lesson. Expecting variety will become a routine: a routine which provides much entertainment and the chance for praise or positive rewards.

Working with 'visuals' in a reading group

It's worth investing in a small whiteboard, which you can put in front of you at the table. Many pupils will benefit from the immediate visual reinforcement that writing words down can bring. Use different coloured marker pens to emphasize spellings, word associations and onset or rhyme patterns.

Psychologically, some pupils like writing on whiteboards themselves because their written efforts can be wiped away instantly. They find this opportunity to wipe away their work emotionally comforting, as more permanent 'writing' puts them on show and makes them feel vulnerable.

Thinking strategies

It will help low-aged readers to improve their reading skills if they analyse the thoughts that pass through their heads as they read.

Learning support teachers can teach these thinking skills and should seek to reinforce them on every possible occasion. For example the list of questions on p. 17 encouraged pupils to ask themselves questions if they get stuck on a difficult word. This is an excellent example of a simple thinking strategy.

Good readers can sense when they are beginning to lose track of what they are reading. As they become aware of the problem, they bring in strategies to compensate for it, for example:

- *Reading ahead.* Skim reading into the text to see whether confusing information can be clarified.
- *Making inferences.* Guessing at the meaning of a word or phrase, on the basis of textual clues and prior knowledge about different genres of writing.
- *Rereading* a difficult section to see if any important detail has been missed.
- *Suspending judgement.* Waiting to see whether the text provides more clues before deciding on a meaning.

Low-aged readers at secondary school are much more likely to panic than to use any of these thinking strategies. They will be struggling to **decode** the text, let alone 'thinking' about the nuances of meaning in what they are reading. Most will be too 'on edge' to keep a constant check of their own reading comprehension. Good readers watch themselves read and are aware when their own state of mind slips into confusion. Poor readers have too much on their mind to notice the moment they stop understanding the text. Learning support teachers have adopted a slang term to describe such mechanical reading without enlightenment. They describe it as 'barking at the text'. It's not a very sensitive term to use when discussing pupils' reading with them, but behind closed doors it is a very apt way of describing the process of reading without understanding.

Sharpening pupils' self-monitoring skills

There are a number of strategies that a reading teacher can use to encourage pupils to think actively as they read. Here are five techniques summarized:

- The teacher models the mental process of getting stuck on a word and shows pupils strategies for solving this problem.
- The teacher shows pupils how to ask themselves about the meaning of the text as they are reading it.
- The teacher gets pupils to form a 'mental picture' of the narrative at certain important moments in the text.
- The teacher gets pupils to construct sentences that summarize the meaning of the text so far.
- The teacher asks pupils to predict what will happen next in the text.

We shall consider each of these methods in turn.

Modelling the mental process

Chapter One. Chelsea Bunny Arrives

Jennifer was in a panic when she drove her old car into Mr Protheroe's garage. She was supposed to be spending Christmas with her Mum. But the car had broken down and there was still a long way to go.

'Stupid thing. Don't do this to me now. I still have presents to buy,' she shouted.

The car mechanic came out. He looked like he had just got out of bed.

The teacher reads this passage aloud to the class, and gets stuck on the word 'mechanic', and deliberately misreading the 'ch' sound and softening it to 'sh'. The hard 'c' at the end of the work is also softened. 'Meshanis' rather than 'mechanic' is the end result.

The teacher explains these reading problems as a stream of consciousness: '"Meshanis" – that doesn't sound right. I'll have to read the sentence again and leave out that word, leave it as a blank.' The teacher reads on aloud to the end of the passage. 'It must be a person because it says he's just got out of bed. What do I know? The story so far involves a car. Who fixes cars? A "meshanis?"'

The teacher reads the difficult sentence again. This time, the strategy of sounding out the word is used: 'Mech – an – '. The teacher segments the beginning of the word into its letter sounds, pretends to suddenly recognise the word and now rereads fluently: 'The car mechanic came out.'

Questioning the meaning

The teacher introduces the passage by saying: 'As I read, I'll ask myself "Is there anything wrong with this story? Is what I'm expecting to happen, still happening in this story? Is this story still making sense? What do I already know about this subject? What's new in this passage?"'

Chelsea Bunny Literacy Workshop – Chapter One

'I came into the room to find him watching Chelsea versus Arsenal. Suddenly he started jumping up and down and banging his head against the sofa.'

'Are you sure you hadn't had too much to drink?'

Mr Protheroe didn't answer and carried on mending the car.

'Bunny seemed to get more excited every time the Chelsea Blues nearly got a goal. But then Arsenal scored with a surprise attack. Bunny let out a terrible squeak. He jumped off the sofa, kicking my glass over. He ran at the screen and "nutted" the picture of the Arsenal players with his head. He went quite crazy when he saw pictures of the Arsenal supporters cheering and waving their scarves.'

'This must be a joke. How could this Bunny do such a thing?'

Mr Protheroe carried on. 'He was shouting and swearing at all the Arsenal fans. I tried to stop him but he took no notice. It was hard to catch him and I couldn't stop him trying to get into the back of the TV set.'

'Go on,' said Jennifer.

'All the time I heard him shouting about getting the Arsenal from behind. Then everything stopped when Chelsea scored an equalizer.'

'Why, why?' Jennifer was quite caught up with the story.

'He suddenly screamed out. Come on you Arsenal, you're not singing any more. I managed to drag him to the tin and shut the lid. He carried on singing and banging his head against the side of the tin.'

The teacher models the thinking strategy of asking oneself a series of self-monitoring questions about meaning while reading a passage. It is shown as a continuous stream of consciousness, but in reality it would be juxtaposed with bouts of decoding text:

So what's happening? A bunny that seems to be watching football? He seems to be getting angry. A man is telling the story and a woman character is asking questions. What's strange? Animals coming to life. So, I'm in some kind of story about magic. I don't know how magic and football could go together? Better read carefully and see how it works. So what's the animal likely to do next? Seems to be interested in a football match. He's wanting to fight the other supporters. Why's she put him in a tin? Why is he banging his head against the side of it?

There are three other strategies that teachers can use to encourage pupils to keep their self-monitoring of what they are reading at a high level.

Forming a mental picture

After the teacher reads a section of narrative, the pupils are asked to visualize a picture in their heads of what is happening. Then they share their image with the rest of the group by talking about it and drawing it.

Constructing summary sentences

Another way of keeping the pupils focused on the meaning of what is being read is to stop after short sections and ask them to write one sentence about the main thing that has happened in the text. With the example of the Chelsea Bunny, these were some of the ideas pupils came up with: 'He's bad and likes fighting.' 'The Bunny has got a bad temper and likes Chelsea.' The same exercise can be done more quickly replacing 'writing' with just 'saying'.

Prediction

By forecasting an opinion of where a narrative will go in the future, a pupil has to take stock of what they currently know and understand about it. So the kind of predictions one might expect a student to give about this story might read like this: 'I think the Bunny will get left in the tin until he learns to behave. Then she will let him out when he stops shouting' or 'I think the Bunny will get so upset in the tin that they will have to let him out. He will probably get really mad if Arsenal score another goal and Chelsea lose the match.' Both predictions are very different but both draw on real knowledge of the story so far, even though they make contrasting use of it.

Assessment

Here is a round-up of the thinking skills that help a pupil read for meaning. Try to consider these in any questioning about a text that you prepare.

* *Summary*. Pupils need to practise summarizing sections of the text. This encourages them to focus on the main ideas in a passage and check their own understanding.
* *Asking questions*. Pupils need to ask questions about what they read. This encourages them to look out for the principal developments in the text.
* *Clarifying*. Pupils need to clarify the meaning of difficult sections of the text, to check their current level of understanding.
* *Predicting*. Using what they have already understood, pupils learn to look ahead and predict how textual meaning will develop.

Using role play in the reading group

Drama through role play is an excellent way of helping your pupils gain access to texts which have a high reading age. It is an excellent strategy to dip in and out of during any guided reading session.
These are some of the benefits to be had from Role Play in reading recovery work:

* It helps bring out the meaning of complex language.
* It's an effective way of encouraging 'reading between the lines' as it helps pupils question character, motivation and plot.
* It's a good way of differentiating difficult texts, where the 'low-aged' reader would struggle to read and understand complex meaning in the narrative.
* It creates useful situations of 'pupil talk'. This type of oracy allows pupils to rehearse ideas, before they try to read them or write them down.
* It's often entertaining and enjoyable – that vital *x* factor ingredient of all literacy recovery work.
* It's often dynamic and unpredictable, which can also stimulate pupils who have felt themselves to be failures with the normal desk-bound curriculum.
* It encourages the students to co-operate and collaborate with their peers. This will be particularly pertinent for struggling readers, who need the support of others pupils as well as their teachers to make the most of lessons.
* Drama encourages the pupils to focus on expressing themselves and communicating with others. It's a great teaching technique for those who have problems with receptive and

expressive language, or who find it hard to understand what they have read. These are *often* problems for our low-aged readers.

As a reading recovery teacher you will often get the chance to work with smaller groups than the mainstream teachers do. So the issues of lack of space and large group sizes are less significant problems for you.

Types of role play interventions

The best types of drama intervention are those which you can use easily with your small groups. You can move in an out of them quickly, so they can be mixed easily with other types of literacy intervention. You can think them up quickly in advance of the lesson or on the spot if you need to. The two types I am going to recommend are teacher and pupil in role.

Teacher in role

The teacher adopts the role of a character in the fiction or non-fiction scenario that you are studying. The pupils are asked to question the character.

Pupils in role

Pupils are asked to come up to the front of the group and assume the role of a character. Then they are interviewed by the teacher and the rest of the class. This process of being put on the spot is sometimes called 'hot seating'.

Benefits of these strategies

Questioning somebody who is in role, or being questioned while in role, is an excellent way for pupils to explore the depth of their subject knowledge.

Role play is a very useful teaching style. It can be successful with either limited or ambitious interventions. You don't have to be a drama expert to use it effectively but you should ask to watch an experienced practitioner use it, before attempting it yourself. Better still, get more extensive training in it.

Working with parents

Reading interventions

It's difficult being any kind of parent, let alone a parent who has a son or daughter who is having persistent difficulty with reading. These parents are having to deal with their own heightened sense of hopes, fears, frustrations and disappointments around their child's learning. They can often shift through a whole gamut of emotions and attitudes when dealing with the objective difficulties their children face. They can blame the child. They can blame the primary school that the child went to. They blame the teachers at your secondary school. They blame you. They blame themselves.

At least, if one or more of these positions is adopted, then you have a clear idea of where you stand. What is more difficult to deal with is the development of a form of apathy and hopelessness – the type of situation where parents say they have given up because they just don't know how to help their child, or where there has clearly been a communication breakdown between parent and teenager, with neither party listening to the other. Sometimes you can be faced with the scenario where the parent claims to be working regularly with the pupil but closer investigation reveals that this isn't happening as consistently as they say.

Two typical examples I've come across are parents who claim that they spend long periods of time helping with homework or say that they sit down and read every night with their child. But such parents often feel pressurized to say what they think is expected of them. The reality is that they cannot force their sons or daughters to co-operate in the learning process any more, and they feel ashamed and humiliated by this.

Sometimes, in their frustration, they fling money at the literacy problem, buying their son or daughter expensive books to read. This is done in the desperate hope that having lots of reading materials will somehow raise reading competency. The books remain unopened on the shelves, gathering dust.

Parents require considerable emotional support in situations where they feel frustration and helplessness about how to help their child, and a learning support teacher is often in a good position to offer it.

Emotional support

Here are some strategies for offering emotional support to parents

If there are perceived problems about the way a subject specialist is teaching a pupil, promise to resolve what you can. Many parents will feel reassured if they see you are prepared to tackle these issues and get back to them. Many problems with individual staff can be resolved easily with a quick chat.

Encourage the parents to focus on the positive about their child. What are their strengths? What is going well? If anything good happens at school for your pupil, it's worth the time to phone or write home about it.

Try to get parents away from a culture of heavy sanctions against their children. They have often started to see disappointing performance at school as a sign of laziness and fecklessness on their son or daughter's part. They resort to punishments such as 'grounding' or stopping pocket money.

Try to connect the reward system you are using with the pupils at school to a parental system of rewards at home. For example ten school merits could lead to a home reward that has been agreed in advance. Manageable rewards might be small financial inducements, new clothes, computer games or money towards a holiday.

It's important to be specific about what leads to what. If rewards are left vague, they are not likely to be given out. You need to encourage the parents into being explicit about what they are going to do.

Above all, be as patient and non-judgemental as you can. Try to listen and give reassurance. You will be asked the question 'My child's dyslexic. What are you doing about it?' again and again and you must be prepared to give a patient and sensible answer that shows you have assessed that individual's reading problems fully and effectively.

When you find yourself in a direct confrontation about the nature of the provision the school is offering, it's important to broker a compromise so that both sides believe there have been concessions. The 'win, win' scenario is the best way forward all round.

Specific strategies

Remember that one of the most important ways you can give parents emotional support is to offer practical advice about how to support their son or daughter in the reading recovery process at home. Parents of secondary-aged pupils have often had years of shame, resentment and frustration around their offspring's literacy prowess. It probably started at primary school when they took a surreptitious look at the books other kids were taking home and measured it unfavourably against their own child's success. Then, the same reading book came home week after week and anxiety levels began to rise. It was the kind of anxiety that fed into jealousy and competitiveness, which in its turn produced more anxiety. Reading sessions at home became a purgatory, with parents and children losing their tempers with each other. This emotional baggage got in the way of a parents supporting their child as effectively as a teacher could in a lesson. You may need to find ways of helping parents enjoy the experience of reading with their child again.

Some simple pointers for parents reading at home

Give parents some simple guidance about the various reading cue strategies they can help their son or daughter with, if they get stuck on an unfamiliar word. They can be same ones you use with the withdrawal group at school, as described in this chapter.

Ask parents to focus on reading for enjoyment. There should be more discussion around meaning and less attention to the technical accuracy of 'text decoding'. Find texts to read that both parent and child can share and enjoy. See p. 49 for a range of low-aged readers currently available for teenagers.

If the teenager gets stuck, encourage parents to give them the word rather than creating negativity by waiting while they struggle over it and get it wrong. Encourage parents to finish any reading session with some praise or reward.

Ask parents to read to their son or daughter some of the time. Just because they're secondary age, it doesn't mean 'being read to' can't be fun.

Further reading

Blum, P., *Chelsea Bunny Literacy Workshop* (Learning Design Limited, telephone 0207 093 4051 or website www.learningdesign.biz). This is an alternative reading scheme for low-aged readers from Year 6 to Year 8. It is particularly suitable for boys. It's used in this chapter to model 'thinking skills'.

Grant, K. (2001) *Supporting Literacy: A Guide for Primary Classroom Assistants* (Routledge Falmer). Despite its specific title, this book is a useful read for all types of literacy support worker. It's written simply and lucidly and has some handy photocopiable materials to support the 'reading aloud' process which could be adapted for work with older pupils.

Durrant, M. (1995) *Creative Strategies for School Problems* (New York: W.W. Norton). An exceptional text that looks at practical case studies in which parents and school work together to overcome deep-seated emotional negativity that some pupils have towards learning.

Airs, J. and Ball, C. (1997) *Key Ideas: Drama* (Folens). This is a guide with many practical ideas for using drama for non-drama specialists.

Chapter 3

Using phonic and non-phonic reinforcement strategies

If you are a learning support teacher with a reading withdrawal group, you have to decide the strategies you use to help pupils who have poor sound-to-letter mapping skills. These poor **phonic** skills inhibit their ability to read unfamiliar words aloud, using the **sub-lexical** strategy that we looked at in Chapter 1.

Historically, there are several major schools of thought on how children learn to read. The first has been described as the 'top down' group. They argue that children learn to recognize new words by reading texts that motivate them. This school of thought is often nicknamed the 'real book' or 'whole language' approach to learning to read. The second major group of opinion is known as the 'bottom up' lobby. They believe that children learn to read primarily by recognizing sound/letter patterns in words and then applying this phonological knowledge to the reading of whole texts. This school of thought believes that teaching phonics is the key to improving reading and that the forty-four grapheme/phoneme correspondences should be taught. Eighty-five per cent of the thirty thousand words used in English are phonetically regular.

Nowadays, many reading experts believe that learning to read is about combining elements from both the above schools of thought. They stress that all readers need instant **sight vocabulary**, an understanding of **context** and the phonological skills to sound out an unfamiliar word when required, using **blending** and **segmenting** techniques. This combined approach forms the basis of the current National Literacy Strategy.

Generally speaking, reading recovery programmes benefit by avoiding the dogma of any particular school of thought on how to teach somebody to improve their reading. Despite this, the stark fact is that the vast majority of low-aged readers at secondary school have poor sound/letter mapping skills. This suggests that they are in great need of a major programme of phonic reinforcement. However my own experience of reading recovery indicates that phonic interventions with older pupils need to be approached with caution. Offering a reading recovery based heavily on phonics, with secondary school students is very different from providing it to young children learning to read for the first time. The older pupils have often had a significant diet of phonic intervention from an early age and it has failed to work effectively. With the onset of the National Literacy Strategy, there is an even greater emphasis on the 'bottom up' phonics approach to learning to read in the early years. Maybe some future low-aged readers will be transformed by this new drive to reinforce their sound-to-letter mapping, but so far this hasn't been the case for many.

Why is the phonic approach with its sounding out of words such a problematic strategy with older pupils?

The main difficulty with phonic teaching strategies are that they tend towards being somewhat abstract and technical. They are abstract in that they offer essentially word-level work, and this alone has no meaningful narrative to go with it. If you read a whole series of words, just because they have a certain phonic pattern, there's no real reading for meaning and little to engage or interest the pupils. Many phonic intervention exercises have been packaged in the form of structured phonics programmes. They can end up being rather boring teaching resources which rely on lessons of endless repetition and reinforcement of sound-to-letter rules. (See Chapter 5.)

If one compares sound-to-letter mapping with the process of making a sound as a note in music, an interesting analogy can be made. You wouldn't try and teach a person the piano just by playing a series of studies that indicate certain intervals of sound, harmonic rules and fingering. The joy of learning music comes from learning how to articulate a musical narrative in form of a melody. The same is true of reading. People can do a few phonic exercises but ultimately they are most stimulated when applying their knowledge in the context of real reading.

So it's often the case that the phonic interventions that work best for secondary pupils are those that revolve around real reading and real writing. For low-aged secondary readers, phonic reinforcement strategies work most effectively when they take account of the following principles.

Guiding principles for phonic interventions in reading groups

- They are used only for short periods of time (two to five minutes of reading group time).
- They are targeted at a particular problem that arises while reading a real text.
- They avoid turning a particular problem into a fully fledged phonics programme.
- They steer clear of reading materials that are particularly primary-school flavoured.

For example, the Mcguiness and Mcguiness reflex reading programme is a typical example of a popular corrective reading course that uses examples geared at younger children. Mcguiness uses images of dogs wearing caps and 'Fat Cat Sat' bingo. Try not to use resources like this on low-aged readers of eleven-plus as it is often emotionally demoralizing for them. The visual images and the wording rub their noses in the fact that they are seriously behind for their age. Reading materials that 'infantalize' the learning of older pupils should be avoided at all costs! One of the most neutral resources currently available for phonics work is Reason and Boote's *Teaching Children with Reading and Spelling*, a valuable resource that I mention often. Although the book is aimed at infant and primary children, the lists of words that match sound and letter rules are without illustrations and are easy to use with older pupils as well. Much of the material in the book is photocopiable. Another useful source of materials is *Improving Literacy Skills for Children with Special Educational Needs* by Heather Duncan and Sarah Parkhouse. Although this is aimed specifically at early and primary years, many of the photocopiable materials on phonics have age-neutral illustrations or no drawing at all.

Useful phonic reinforcement reading strategies

The following strategies can encourage low-aged readers at secondary school to improve their sound to letter mapping skills. They make the biggest impact if they are used with the four guiding principles for secondary school phonic intervention mentioned above.

Rapid segmenting and blending in a familiar text

To summarize, segmenting means splitting a word down through letter combinations into its sounds; blending means putting a word together by moulding its sounds back into letter combinations. See the fuller definitions in the glossary at the end of the book and a practical example below of using the two skills with the word 'mechanic'.

Rather than following stepped phonics programmes, it's often best to practise sound-to-letter mapping on a word that the pupils have already read successfully in a text they have selected for themselves. With words the pupil already knows, the anxiety is taken out of practising sound-to-letter mapping. Pupils are already confident they can say the word. So it's a good place to start a close focus on the way sound and letters relate. This principle can be extended to other words with a similar pattern or different forms of the same word. For example 'mechanical' could become 'mechanically' or 'mechanism'.

Rapid segmenting and blending with unfamiliar words

On some occasions the same exercises can be done with a word that the pupil is finding difficult to read. Although this causes more anxiety, it's still important to do it occasionally as sounding out words is a vital reading sub-skill.

The teacher covers the word with a finger, then uncovers part of the word – sometimes the beginning, sometimes the end – sometimes keeping two fingers on the word, so that the middle is left uncovered. This gets the pupil to practise segmenting a word. Finally, the pupil is given the opportunity to blend the whole word back together, as demonstrated in the example of the word 'mechanic' here.

mec	han	ic
mec	han	ic
mec	han	ic

Ask the pupils to clap the number of syllables that they are saying and count them out. This helps them gain a sense of sound and rhythm around the way a word is put together.

| mech | an | ic |
| 1 | 2 | 3 |

Instruct the pupils to say the second syllable, the third syllable etc. of the word, based on what was their first, second or third clap. Give the pupils a word they know or pick on a word that you know they've got stuck on. Ask them to break it down into its *phonemes* (sound syllables).

Point out a word within a word as that can help in the segmenting process. For example, the word 'repetition' contains the word 'pet' or 'tit' or the longer word 'petition'.

Build up a word gradually, by uncovering it from under your finger:

co	mpetition
com	petition
comp	etition
compet	ition
competit	ion
competition

Now cover up the word with your finger up to 'comp'. Ask the pupil to say the second half of the word and then uncover the first half of the word and get them to blend the whole word together.

As the teacher, you can play with the sound/letter patterns in the word, covering up parts of the words. The pupils will end up getting a grilling on every sound in the word.

Good points about blending and segmenting exercises:

- They are easy to use – any word, any sentence in any text at any time.
- They can be used very quickly – a swift phonological exercise around one phoneme in a word (thirty seconds), then back to the text.
- They are flexible. You can break a word down and roll it back together again and then test the pupils' understanding of sound/letter mapping in the word by going over the parts of the word in all sorts of order. You could create a list of words with similar sound/letter maps and look at them as well. But it can still be a short intervention of less than three minutes.
- They are based around text you are actually reading so it's easier to motivate the student to take the exercise seriously, persuading them that these are words they really need.

- You can also do these exercises with words pupils can already read, so they are more comfortable about segmenting into some sound/letter patterns.
- You can switch quickly from phonic intervention back to the text.

Possible drawbacks:

- Every time you stop and digress on a short phonic intervention with a pupil, others in the group, even the pupil you are working with, may lose the momentum of the story line and get confused or restive.
- A light-touch intervention may be too light to improve the phonological skills of many low-aged secondary readers. You may need to consider an intensive phonics programme and risk alienating a pupil with the technical abstract word work that it entails. If you go down this path, try to take it in small steps with lots of rewards.

Sound diagrams and phonic games

Secondary pupils respond well to games around phonological processing – especially when linked to competition and reward. The most popular game I've used gives them letter sounds from the alphabet and is called a Boggle diagram. The pupils have to make up words from the diagram within a set time limit and there are several common variations of the game.

Here are some of the types I've seen used most with older pupils.

Boggle diagram 1

g	r	t
e	ch	a

The pupils are asked to make up as many words as they can from the letter sounds on this diagram. They are allowed to use the letters as many times as they want. Letters are not permitted if they are not on the diagram, and letter combinations such as *ch* cannot be split up and used seperately. Here are some of the likely examples: each, tar, tag, gear, gag, chat, eat and tag.

Boggle diagram 2

r	l	p
i	sh	ch

Pupils are asked to make up as many words as they can, using these letters to *begin* words – at least three words from each letter box. Likely examples include: rat, rap, rain, pat, pain, pet, lap, lorry, lazy etc.

Boggle diagram 3

ing	tion
ch	ck

Pupils are asked to make up as many words as they can, using the sounds in the diagram as *word endings*. Here are some examples: truck, back, such, much, waiting, looking, seeing, each, station, relation, position.

Some general rules for Boggle diagrams:

- Set a time limit.
- Give two marks for a correct answer of a simple word. One mark for writing the word itself and one mark for an explanation of what it means.
- Give four marks for correct answer to a complex word, two marks for writing the word itself and another two for describing accurately what it means. This will encourage pupils to experiment with more sophisticated language and vocabulary.
- Take a mark off a pupil who makes up a word or spells a word wrong.

When working with Boggle diagrams, pupils can come up and write their answers on a whiteboard. The exercise is a wonderful starting point for the teacher to digress into the various sound-to-letter mappings in English. Often it's possible to identify onset and rhyme pattern. The teacher can also use the exercise to explore the meaning of words. Some benefits of Boggle diagrams are:

- They encourage pupils to dig deeply into their vocabulary, especially when they get more marks for risking a complex word.
- They encourage pupils to take risks with their phonological awareness as they try and add words to their lists.
- They are prompted by the Boggle diagram formula to find patterns of words from which they can either change the '**onset**' or the '**rime**'.
- They are given a reason for wanting to spell a word correctly – they want to win the game.
- They are encouraged to consider the relationship between certain sounds and letter combinations.
- They do all the above as part of a game, hardly noticing they are doing abstract phonics work.

Phonics card games and other board games

Anything that involves an element of entertainment and competition is likely to draw in older pupils. The Boggle games are a quick and easy way of doing this, as are games such as Scrabble and Word Bingo. A company called Gamz has produced a series of simple card games around phonological processing for small groups of up to four players. The games work on simple card-game principles and players use letter combinations to follow on in the suit before them. They have to recite the words or letter strings they are creating. Good points of the games are:

- Seeing, speaking and hearing are involved.
- Playing a competitive game is entertaining.
- It's a painless way to explore sound-to-letter mapping.
- You can do it for a short time, so it's only a part of any lesson.

Short phonic interventions around a pupil's own writing

The pupil's writing is another good source for quick sound/letter exercises. If the intervention is based around words that pupils want to communicate with in writing, they are much more likely to want to read them back properly.

A teacher can make a list of key words that the pupils have decided to use in their writing. The words can be a basis for the blending or segmenting 'reading aloud' exercises described above.

'Intellectualizing' phonics

Some secondary pupils respond positively to looking at phonics as though it were a specialized subject on the curriculum such as history, geography or maybe the algebra section of maths. They are comfortable taking on the notion that they need to learn about the linguistic rules of English by taking on board the meaning of words such as 'blending', 'lexical' etc. Such pupils seem more comfortable improving their own reading when they have an intellectual understanding of the reading process itself. Obviously this is the kind of approach that the National Literacy Strategy is trying to encourage in children much younger than secondary school age. If you have pupils that respond to this approach, make the most of it.

The limitations of this approach are that many pupils don't respond to the rules and regulations of the phonics system. They fight shy of having any further knowledge of phonics, either as abstract knowledge or when applied to their own reading. Some secondary pupils respond to learning about phonological processing as an objective body of knowledge but they still shrink from applying the rules to their own reading.

Non-phonic reinforcement: strategies to build sight vocabulary

We have already established that many secondary low-aged readers have poor phonological processing skills. However, a substantial number of these do not respond to strategies designed to improve their sound-to-letter mapping. So the learning support teacher has to look to alternative methods of getting them to read a wider range of words, without involving 'sounding out'.

We need to consider the dual route model and look for strategies that encourage pupils to improve the **lexical** route to reading that we looked at on p. 6. The lexical route is the process by which a reader recognizes a whole word immediately, without the need to break it down into its sounds – instantaneous word recognition or **sight vocabulary**.

If your low-aged reader is reluctant to work on phonics, you might consider intervention techniques that encourage expanded memory for whole words. Essentially, you will be prompting the pupils to use their lexical rather than their sub-lexical route to reading more fluently and efficiently.

Expanding the pupil's store

Words that a pupil wants to use are the ones they are likely to find relevant to remember. This is the golden rule for building sight vocabulary. Here are some ideas:

- Use the pupils' own writing. Pick out words that they have used and get them to keep a dictionary of personal-interest words.
- Write a narrative with the pupil. Ask them to choose a word they want to use, and get them to write it into a personal dictionary.
- Spend time building up lists of subject specific words that pupils are going to need in their lessons. So there would be a history list, a science list and a technology list. This method works particularly well if you are working alongside the pupil as in-class support in those particular lessons every week.
- Make sure that they have spontaneous recognition of a basic list of the most commonly used words as illustrated in the following table. The highest-frequency words can make up to fifty per cent of most texts. They are the cement in the bricks of the wall. If pupils know these words really well, it will ease their reading problems.

Here is the list of the most high-frequency words:

A he in it of the to went and I is my that then was with am at for had have his me out see some they we are come go has her little one saw she there this when about all as back because but call can did down get here into like look make next now old once our put so their three today two up were will after an away be big by came could do from out him last live made new not off on other over said take them time too us very what you

Reinforcement techniques to build

- Write down the target word in a personal dictionary or subject word list. Read the word with the pupil but don't ask them to focus on the phonetic structure of the word if that demotivates them.
- Ask the pupil to pick out any distinguishing visual features for the word or letter combinations – for example words within a word, such as 'e*clip*se' or 'marri*age*'.
- Discuss the meaning of the word.
- Mime the word. For example, the teacher could mime the word 'kick' and encourage the pupil to do the same. This short role play helps to secure the word in the pupil's memory. Some pupils will find other **kinaesthetic** learning techniques useful – for example writing the difficult word down by tracing it on an imaginary whiteboard in the air.
- Pupils with strong visual memories may find colouring a letter combination in a word may help them recognize the same word when they try to read it again. For example 'lamb' with its silent *b* may be memorable if the poor reader remembers seeing it coloured with green dots.
- Make up sentences using the word in its context. This can be an oral or written exercise.
- Return to the list for reinforcement next session, for a few minutes.
- Return yet again for reinforcement in a regular monthly test – building on an ever longer list.
- Link the reinforcement process to verbal praise and rewards. There should be a sense of fun about the pupil increasing the range of words they recognize and remember how to read.
- Try to consider the basic principle that many pupils begin to absorb and retain more sight vocabulary if you encourage them to learn to spell the words as they go along. Chapter 7 looks at how highly personalized spelling methods that rely on visual, aural and kinaesthetic learning styles can help significantly in fixing a word in a pupil's mind.
- Don't spend too long on strategies for improving sight vocabulary in one of your reading recovery sessions. Sight vocabulary must not be allowed to dominate the process of engaging with a text, and a mixed bag of interventions is always more entertaining for the pupil than the monotonous concentration on any one thing for too long.

Reinforcement strategies around the meaning of words

Some pupils will need their learning support teacher to focus on the problems they have in remembering the meaning of words they are trying to learn. This can often be a problem when the pupil is quite capable of reading a word fluently.

Language difficulties fall into two broad categories: difficulties in understanding (receiving language from other people) and difficulties in speaking (expressing thoughts and feelings to other people). Many low-aged readers at secondary school have both.

Symptoms of difficulties in understanding (receptive language) are likely to include limited vocabulary and frequent difficulties in understanding the meaning of words in class. This can lead to problems with following instructions and understanding what has been read.

Symptoms of difficulties in speaking (expressive language) are likely to include one or more of the following:

- disordered speech that lacks the usual structures
- words that are missed out or put together in the wrong order
- stammering and hesitation
- limited vocabulary

Some pupils are simply slower than others at acquiring the range of language they need. Others have particular problems with certain aspects of their language development. By the time they are at secondary school, very few pupils get the opportunity to meet a speech and language therapist. Language work will inevitably come from the learning support teacher. Some of these pupils read effectively, in that they can decode text very fluently but they may not necessarily understand what they are reading. They are prone to 'barking at the text', the phrase we have used to describe pupils who read without comprehension.

Ten tips for working with pupils with language impairment

Language impairment is a complex specialism, and I would recommend you to get specialist help with a pupil whom you are finding hard to help. The following points offer general guidance in working with pupils who fall into this category of language difficulty.

- Try to make eye contact with your pupil – not every time you speak to them, as this would be intimidating, but when you want them to concentrate very hard on the meaning of words. They may need to watch you as well as listen to you if they are to understand language they find difficult. You may need to stop them fiddling with pens, pencils and bags, a common displacement activity when pupils feel under pressure.
- Highlight and explain key words for a specialist topic before you encounter them in a text. (This is good practice for all pupils with literacy difficulties.) Remember that you will probably need to look at some general words as well as subject-specific ones.
- When communicating, try to speak using short simple sentences. Monitor your own speech by thinking about the way you are expressing something as you actually say it. Be prepared to rephrase the sentence by changing the one or two words that could be causing confusion.
- Give pupils time to respond to what you've asked. Don't let yourself dominate the interaction and do all the talking.
- Don't try to correct too much of what the pupil says. Try and concentrate on one aspect of their speech to improve upon. Let them know what you are focusing on.
- Encourage pupils to expand their answers. Ask gently for more detail or probe them by asking them to explain the meaning of a particular word or phrase in a different way.
- Ask pupils how a character might be feeling at a particular point in the narrative. Ask them to predict ahead into the narrative.
- Find out whether there is a learning style that a pupil responds well to. For example, a film of a play may 'unlock' them more than reading the play itself. Maybe speech will flow more freely if your student has more visual, aural or 'hands-on' input in their lesson with you. Drama and role play are very effective: we looked at their potential in Chapter 2.
- Every so often, model the answer to a question yourself. It will give a good oral example to your pupil.
- Give lots of praise to keep pupils feeling relaxed and pleased with their own progress.

Further reading and resources

Reason, R. and Boote, R. (1994) *Helping Children with Reading and Spelling: A Special Needs Manual* (Routledge). This book often provides a further source of reading, even though it is geared at younger pupils. The phonics tables for the various stages of reading that Reason and Boote suggest are an excellent resource if you want to make the kind of 'light-touch' phonological intervention suggested in this chapter from lists already published.

Mcguiness, C. and Mcguiness, G. (1998) *Reading Reflex: The Foolproof Phono-grafix Method for Teaching Your Child to Read* (Penguin). This is one of the most popular phonic-based approaches to learning to read. It is not an approach that I think works well with secondary school pupils, but it has some tables and resources with some useful ideas for making a 'light-touch' intervention. Material used from this text will need adaptation to break the 'young child' feel.

Gamz is the company which makes a number of useful phonological word card games. Its website address is http://www.gamzuk.com and the email enquiry site is enquiry@gamzuk.com.

Wyse, D. and Jones, R. (2001) *Teaching English, Language and Literacy* (Routledge/Falmer). This has an excellent section on the debate around the importance of phonics in the reading process.

This is an excellent overview to the research around teaching phonic skills, although it is aimed at primary rather than secondary work. The reading lists provide many detailed references.

Martin, D. (2000) *Teaching Children with Speech and Language Difficulties* (Fulton). A good introductory book, which will give you more practical ideas about how to help pupils who find it hard to use language.

Literacy Progress Units Level Two (DFES, 2001). These are phonics teaching programmes that you can download from the website on www.standards.dfes.gov.uk/keystage3/publications. They contain some useful checklists of sound-to-letter combinations with exercises. All free of charge and good for dipping in and out of.

Chapter 4

Support in mainstream lessons

It's vital to remember that the key to effective support lies in building a partnership between learning support and secondary subject staff. Effective learning support teachers will have asked themselves the following key questions and be working on practical answers to them in their daily in-class support work in the school:

Can I find a way of encouraging mainstream subject teachers to think of the low-aged readers in the class as they prepare their lessons?

Can I find a way of interpreting the available lesson materials to make them work better for struggling readers?

In-class support in the context of the National Literacy Strategy

The National Literacy Strategy (NLS) has put literacy into the heart of the Curriculum for the foreseeable future. At secondary school level it has served the useful role of extending responsibility for literacy to all curriculum subjects and not just English. Theoretically, every teacher is a teacher of literacy. The NLS has defined very accurately what a literate child should be able to do and is in the process of creating a whole range or resources that can help both mainstream and learning support teachers in their work.

As the NLS extends into secondary schools for pupils in Years 7 to 9, it brings with it the same recommended structure as the literacy hour at primary school. Secondary teachers of English following the Framework Document will have a short starter activity of ten minutes. Based on some feature of spelling, grammar or language work, the starter is supposed to be a 'pacey' interaction between teacher and class. The central section of the lesson is led by the teacher, introducing a linguistic idea or maybe modelling a piece of writing. The pupils then work as a whole class or divide into groups. A short ten-minute reinforcement of the main objectives of the lesson takes place at the end, in a plenary session.

The central section of the lesson, where it is suggested that the class can be divided into groups, offers the best opportunities for learning support teachers to work with low-aged readers. The NLS recommends that guided reading should take place in this half-hour slot. 'Guided reading' is a scenario in which the pupils divide into groups to read and interrogate a text for meaning. The subject mainstream teacher is supposed to spend a large amount of time with one group of pupils, while the others work independently. This creates the chance for a learning support teacher to work closely with a group of low-aged readers, using the strategies for assessment and intervention I have suggested in the earlier sections of the book, either as fully fledged reading withdrawal from the room or by creating a separate group within the classroom itself. If a learning support teacher is allowed to work with the same group of low-aged readers every lesson, there will be opportunities for the support teacher to differentiate the specialist subject materials and make them more accessible for their weak readers.

Building relationships with mainstream subject teachers

For this kind of teaching and learning scenario to occur, the learning support teacher needs to build up a trusting and flexible working relationship with mainstream subject teachers. A central part of this working partnership is the information they share about the reading difficulties of the target pupils and the strategies they adopt together to accommodate them effectively.

The Individual Education Plan and reading recovery

Traditionally, the main tool for communication under the Special Needs Code of Practice is the Individual Education Plan (IEP). This is supposed to offer help and advice to teachers about the best ways of supporting the individual pupil's difficulty. It outlines a personal teaching and learning programme with agreed targets for the pupil. The plan is implemented and monitored by the classroom teachers, with the help of a Learning Support Team.

IEPs are probably a much more effective tool at primary than at secondary school level. One class teacher works with the pupil for most of the school day. This enables the learning support teacher to work closely with one professional, to determine a sensible IEP for a pupil. But at secondary school there are at least ten subject teachers, all with their own classroom teaching style and personality. It is very difficult for one learning support teacher to create an educational plan with so many people. In his 2001 article in the *British Journal of Special Education*, Tony Lingard, a Special Educational Needs Co-ordinator in a large secondary school in Cornwall, exposed this fact very vividly when an extensive survey that he did revealed that most secondary Sencos in Cornwall felt that the IEPs they wrote were having very little impact on improving learning. They reported to him that most subject teachers didn't read or contribute to IEPs properly, because they did not prioritize them above the other pieces of assessment data they received. In Lingard's 2001 survey, secondary Sencos were asked whether time spent writing and administering IEPs would be better spent on direct pupil support. Not surprisingly, twenty-four out of twenty-six said that it would!

Disseminating information to ten subject teachers at a secondary school is much less effective than preparing an IEP with one class teacher in a primary: single ownership of a plan is much easier to set up meaningfully at primary school than multi-ownership at secondary. Whilst you may be fortunate to work in a secondary school where IEPs work brilliantly and involve all subject teachers, many teachers will be more familiar with the less than perfect setup I have just described.

The learning support teacher also needs to consider that secondary subject teachers don't know the pupils in the same way as one primary class teacher, who spends the whole day with the class. In terms of reading recovery for pupils, the tradition of seeing oneself as a 'teacher of literacy' is not as strong at secondary school as it is at primary. Whereas the literacy hour has consolidated the role of the primary school teacher as a teacher of reading, most secondary school teachers still see themselves as a teacher of subjects rather than literacy despite the fond wishes of the NLS.

So learning support teachers in secondary schools need to find their own practical ways of communicating with the mainstream staff and minimizing reliance on IEPs. Multiple target-setting on paper does not help pupils improve their reading skills if it becomes a substitute for building up practical strategies for supporting struggling readers with their secondary subject teachers. To suggest that the writing of many types of IEP at secondary school is a waste of valuable time may shock many of the readers of this book. The whole government strategy for supporting pupils with learning difficulties around reading is anchored on the concept of individual target-setting documents. I have never read a book on learning support that hasn't considered the most effective way of doing it rather than questioning whether it should be done at all. However, I am suggesting that, given the limited time in a school day, you need to prioritize other means of helping your students improve their literacy skills if you are to have maximum impact. Creating a paper trail of IEPs may look impressive when inspectors come in on an auditing exercise, but it often becomes a poor substitute for the real work of differentiating the curriculum for low-aged readers and for training staff thoroughly about how to meet their needs.

Better ways of planning reading support

Try to talk to subject teachers about the needs of the pupil – rather than write lists of targets for them to meet. Informal 'snatched' communications of a minute here and there are more effective than time-consuming form-filling. It is even better if you can create formal meeting time, although in the terrible bustle of the school day this is seldom possible.

The Special Needs Co-ordinator can make a big difference to what subject staff do in the classroom by training groups of staff on user-friendly types of differentiation. To some extent you can do that same thing on a regular basis with the mainstream staff you work with if you model these techniques with the pupils you work with in their lessons. (See Chapter 6.)

Training needs to be carried out when a teacher is new to the school, but departments also need 'refreshing' regularly. Regular training of staff rather than writing IEPs should be the driving engine for improving struggling pupils' literacy levels.

Drop-in lunchtime sessions can be a good idea. Support teachers with literacy expertise can pass ideas on to mainstream teachers as they come and go from the staffroom. Teachers get used to knowing where and when to find help and advice without having to fill in or read dreaded bits of paper.

If you are going to use an IEP to describe strategies for reading intervention, it cuts down on paper work to try to identify *groups* of pupils with the same types of literacy problems in one class. This helps the teachers get their minds more focused on the general teaching issues that arise for a specific section of their class. The New Code of Practice encourages this kind of approach. It describes it as a Group Education Plan.

Resistance to in-class literacy support

The silent teaching syndrome

One of the biggest barriers to effective collaboration that support teachers frequently encounter in the main stream classroom is the quest for 'silent working' by some teachers. Long periods of teacher talk are followed by a 'battening down of the hatches' and silent written work. Whilst concentrating in complete silence may be a good thing for many members of the class, the kind of pupils you are likely to be supporting will probably need some careful one-to-one preparation to get them ready to do any extended written task.

But the kind of oral interactions which can help pupils with poor reading skills have to be conducted in a whisper. In some classes all 'talk' is frowned upon by the authoritarian subject teacher. As one support teacher so accurately summed it up: 'I feel similar to the humming radiator on the floor, that's about as useful and animate as I'm allowed to become.'

The embarrassed teaching syndrome

Not all teachers wish to create a totally silent classroom but they are slightly embarrassed at having another teacher in the room. They don't know how to make the most of having a learning support teacher or assistant there. Such teachers need very specific guidance about how to 'let you into the lesson'. This guidance can come from you directly, supported by the Head of Learning Support. The best schools have a clear policy on how subject teachers and learning support staff can interact, but many still need you to interpret the guidance practically and sensibly in your daily relationships.

How to maximize the role of a learning support teacher in the mainstream classroom

Try to work with teachers who are enthusiastic about having extra support. It's unlikely that you can ever be so inspirational as to change the negative way that some teachers feel about having you in the room. They will always work in a regimented and autocratic way. So take the line of least resistance.

Once you get to know how sympathetic your teachers are to working collaboratively with you, meet with them formally or informally to discuss the input you can make to their next lesson. But don't put too many demands on their advanced planning, as they're probably having to deal with a lot of classes and a lot of daily friction generated in them.

Ask your mainstream teacher to introduce you to the class pupils properly, so everybody knows you are there for an important purpose to help all the pupils in that class. It's best that your special relationship to weak readers isn't stated too overtly, to avoid a negative spotlight on their difficulties.

Experiment with a number of working practices. On some occasions get the pupils who need literacy support in a little group around you, if you are offering in-class support. On other occasions you should consider taking the pupils out of class, one-to-one, or sometimes in small groups, if you want to reinforce some of the reading skills that the rest of the class already have. Encourage the whole-class teacher to be flexible about letting you do this. If you have built up a good working relationship with that teacher, this is much easier to set up.

Offer to simplify work on the spot, during the lesson or, if you have the time, before the next lesson. Most teachers love the input of teaching materials that they can use again and again with other classes. (See Chapter 6 for techniques for simplifying dense texts.)

Ask whether you can go round the room and mark or annotate work for literacy skills. It will allow you to model good practice for the classroom teacher as well as to take the weight of marking for literacy from their shoulders alone. Having two people marking work is a quicker way of getting through more books and gives individual pupils more teacher time.

Encourage your classroom teacher to give you freedom to help all the pupils from time to time, whatever their literacy needs. It's good to be like a bee pollinating all the flowers, not just the ones that are not doing so well. It will raise your status as an adult with knowledge and expertise amongst all the pupils. Even more importantly, it will take the spotlight off pupils with weak literacy. They are already likely to be ashamed and embarrassed about being singled out for help a lot of the time.

There are useful ways in which you can support a subject teacher while they teach from the front. Some whole-class teachers can draw and write as they speak to or ask questions of a class, but many find more than one activity at a time difficult. If your whole-class teacher is busy explaining something, you could write key words and phrases on the board. You could do a flow diagram to represent these ideas. Such activities will reinforce the literacy content of the lesson and help the poorer readers access the subject matter better. This kind of impromptu arrangement for working should be exploited, whenever possible.

Ultimately, it's very good for your status as a teacher to team-teach on some occasions. If you lead the lesson, the mainstream teacher can take the role of support teacher and this gives them hands-on experience of what the practical issues are in supporting the pupils with literacy difficulties.

The role of the Special Educational Needs Co-ordinator, literacy co-ordinator and senior management

When you experience difficulties working with a particular member of the mainstream staff or a pupil, the Special Educational Needs Co-ordinator will be a key player in helping you resolve them. Special Educational Needs Co-ordinators (Sencos) are likely to line-manage the literacy recovery work for low-aged readers in the school. They may have a senior management role. But often they are not in the leadership team and have a line manager who is responsible for literacy across the curriculum and all forms of student support in the school. If that senior person is knowledgeable and supportive, they can encourage the majority of teachers in the school to work positively with literacy support staff. A good senior line manager may even find a way for you to have proper formal meeting times with the mainstream subject staff you work with.

The most efficient schools build a literacy support meeting into their regular meeting cycle. Even with the best intentions, it is almost impossible to build in a planning slot between every support teacher and each of the subject teachers they work with in the week. But closer relationships between staff can be fostered by putting a specific member of the reading recovery team in a particular department. The relationship is encouraged further if that learning support teacher goes to departmental meetings and has as much of their timetable as possible with members of staff from that department.

Regular problems

Here are some regular problems cited by learning support teachers in secondary schools:

PROBLEM **?**

Secondary school pupils get increasingly ashamed of their literacy difficulties and they are more and more likely to shun help from learning support teachers.

SOLUTION **✓**

In lessons where the literacy support and mainstream teacher have a good rapport, the literacy support can be given to everybody. The support teacher will move freely around the room and the mainstream teacher will encourage all pupils to expect help from them. This does a lot to break down the stigma of 'being helped'.

PROBLEM **?**

As a learning support teacher, I am timetabled to go to only one English GCSE lesson a week with my Year 10 group. I haven't got more than a hazy idea what has happened in the other three hours of lesson time, so I can't help my pupils properly.

SOLUTION **✓**

Timetable constraints in secondary schools do make this a common situation. Wherever possible, try to support the same pupils and the same teacher for most of the subject lessons in a week so you can keep up with what is going on. Supporting a few colleagues, who are keen for you to be there, in as many of their lessons as possible is a more productive way of delivering effective literacy support than following an individual pupil through many different subject lessons.

PROBLEM **?**

Miss Brown is a complete tyrant. The pupils are so frightened of her that there's this deathly silence in the room. If anyone speaks, she glares at them. As the learning support teacher, responsible for improving literacy, I feel as frightened to speak as the pupils, so I can't help differentiate the curriculum for pupils with weak literacy skills.

SOLUTION **✓**

There's no easy solution to this one. You must ask yourself the important question: Is this the behaviour of a colleague in a rogue minority or the general attitude of a lot of the staff? If that teacher is part of a small minority, you could try and tackle it in the following ways.

- Ask Miss Brown whether you can take the 'low-aged' readers out of the room, so that you can work with them in a room where talking is not going to be a problem.

---

continued

- Ask Miss Brown whether you can gather key pupils around you and speak to them for a period of time in the lesson.
- Get your head of department to talk on your behalf to that colleague or to their line manager.
- Ask your head of department to ask senior management in the school to reiterate to all staff the ways in which literacy recovery work is supposed to take place in the classrooms.
- Ask to be moved to another class. There's no point sitting in silence in a lesson because you can't help anybody.

If the problem of 'silent classrooms' in which literacy support staff are unable to make a sound is a general school problem, you should lobby for a change of policy via your line manager. Otherwise go for the points of least resistance – many teachers will be very glad of your support and help with the pupils in their lessons.

PROBLEM **?**

The mainstream teacher has no control of the lesson. There is constant friction and confrontation. None of the pupils I'm supposed to be helping with their weak reading will work with me.

SOLUTION ✓

Like the 'silent classroom' this is not an easy situation. Both situations are very bad for reading recovery work.

- See whether you can get your group of targeted pupils out of the class, so you can work with them in a room where you, not your mainstream teacher, establishes behaviour boundaries.
- Talk to the mainstream teacher and try to agree a strategy where you offer specific support on managing behaviour each lesson.
- Whatever you do, don't try to take over the management of the class as this will fatally undermine your relationship with that mainstream teacher.
- If neither 1 nor 2 seems possible, it's your duty to let your head of department know that there are major problems in the lesson.
- If there's no solution to the problems, get permission to move on to another class where effective literacy support can be given to the same pupils.

Further reading

Garner, P. and Dwfor Davies, J. (2001) *Introducing Special Educational Needs* (Fulton). A good introductory guide explaining the role of all the various stake-holders in the field of Special Educational Needs. The writers look at the role of key players such as classroom teacher, Special Needs Co-ordinator and parents. The book outlines 'model' Special Needs school policy and Individual Education Planning. The reality of school life is sometimes very different!

Lingard, Tony (2001) 'Does the code of practice help secondary school Sencos to improve learning?', *British Journal of Special Education*, vol. 28 no. 4 (December). This article makes fascinating reading for all those secondary learning support teachers and Sencos who have felt there is something seriously wrong with the target-setting and review agenda of learning support work. Tony Lingard's study brings some proper research to bear on the matter.

British Dyslexia Association (2003) *Achieving Dyslexia-friendly Schools*, third edition. There is plenty of good advice in this information pack about the kinds of policy and practice that a school needs to establish to help its dyslexic pupils. The tips for secondary school teachers are very sensible. However, some of the messages of 'zero tolerance' of teachers' failure to cater for dyslexic pupils would be best toned down a bit, if learning support teachers want to build up harmonious relationships with mainstream subject teachers. According to this document, failure of the dyslexic child to learn is always the failure of the teaching strategy and never the pupil. Whilst, in its purest form, this is probably true, it is not a good way of approaching classroom teachers who already have a lot of challenges to deal with and won't thank you for persisting with a point like this when they have had a difficult lesson.

Basic Skills Agency (1998) What Works in Secondary Schools? Catching Up with Basic Skills. This booklet is based on a research project on literacy that the Basic Skills Agency conducted in just over one hundred secondary schools nationwide. It looked at the strategies that schools needed to take on board to improve reading and spelling skills. The results of this analysis are very interesting and demonstrate the importance of good working relations between support staff and mainstream teachers as well as of working with parents. The project looked at the kind of reading withdrawal intervention that worked best. This document is available free from the Basic Skills Agency at Commonwealth House, 1–19 New Oxford Street WC1A 1NU, telephone 0207 405 4017.

Chapter 5

Finding resources

This chapter looks at resources produced for struggling readers by the government and by commercial publishers. The DFES has a main offering of the Literacy Progress Units and the commercial publishers market corrective reading schemes and fiction and non-fiction reading books.

The Literacy Progress Units

The Literacy Progress Units, nicknamed 'Catch-Up' by schools, represent a potentially useful resource for teachers, teaching assistants and other literacy workers who are working regularly with a small group of pupils. They are the DFES's attempt to provide materials for teachers working on literacy recovery. They are aimed at the very top end of the 'low-aged readers' group in secondary school, and so are only of limited use to the group of struggling readers that most learning support staff are asked to work with.

Organization of the Literacy Progress Units

The organization of Literary Progress Units has improved a lot since the Draft Progress Units of 2000. There are currently six literacy progress units. They are *Writing Organisation*, *Information Retrieval*, *Spelling*, *Reading between the Lines*, *Phonics* and *Sentences*. Each unit is divided into eighteen sessions, which are meant to last exactly twenty minutes. It should be possible to do three sessions a week and complete a unit in six weeks.

The Literacy Progress Units can be run in the school day during lesson time. But equally they can be run at lunchtime or after school. The literacy professionals who run them will need extra time to plan in advance. There are many resources to photocopy, cut up and stick together before the sessions. The Progress Unit guidelines warn that it is vital to have everything prepared in advance or the momentum of the lessons will be compromised.

Purpose of the Literacy Progress Units

The Units are to be taught by all types of literacy support workers – not just fully trained teachers. The sessions are designed for groups of up to eight students. They work around a very explicit formula for each session

* *Remember* (identification of prior knowledge and key objectives)
* *Model* (teacher demonstration of process)
* *Try* (shared exploration through activity)
* *Apply* (scaffolded pupil application on new learning)
* *Secure* (consolidation through discussion/activity).

Here are some suggestions for making the best use of the Progress Units:

- Give yourself time to sit down with the Progress Units and pick out things that look interesting.
- Insist on time to work with another literacy professional in preparing Progress Unit material. Two people discussing the material will bring more out of it than one person working alone.
- You'll need some basic equipment – overhead projector is mentioned most often.
- Dip in and out of the units and the exercises on offer.
- When you've found a good exercise that works, try to use it repeatedly so that you get really confident with it. You could use the skills it promotes to teach different material of your own.
- To avoid the boredom factor, experiment with running a couple of Progress Units at the same time. This gives you the variety of dipping into different types of material. This would be particularly helpful when you are doing somethng such as phonics.
- When you have found a useful exercise on reading, writing or spelling, follow it up with further practice around a real text, ideally something the pupils are using in English or another lesson. Reinforce and consolidate what the Progress Unit has started.
- Allow more time than the twenty minutes by encouraging the pupils to read aloud and improve their fluency and 'reading for meaning' skills. Encourage them to consolidate their understanding of what's going on by interrogating some of the texts more fully. (The thinking skill strategies recommended in Chapter 2 are useful.)
- Allow more time for you to read aloud to the class from the units. This is a strategy which is suggested in the units from time to time, but it's useful to do it more frequently. The pupils will learn a lot from the way that you use tone and expression. Most of your pupils have a long way to go to improve their confidence and reading fluency with difficult texts.

Level Two Progress Units

At the time of writing this chapter, National Curriculum Level Two Progress Units have become available from the DFES Standards website, www.standards.dfes.gov.uk/keystage3/publications. They can be downloaded and printed out in their entirety. The Units contain a lot of teacher resources that are pitched at a level more suitable for secondary school pupils with significant literacy difficulties. Units included are *Phonics, Handwriting and Presentation. Writing Non-fiction* and *Reading Non-fiction* are in the pipeline. The website also displays a miscue analysis guide to assessing reading, very similar to the one explained in Chapter 1 above. All these internet materials are in the process of being piloted and developed but they offer more long-term potential to literacy recovery pupils than the current Level 3 Units.

Overall assessment

The best thing about the Progress Units is the way they identify the concepts and skills pupils need to improve their reading and writing. What they fail to do convincingly is to give teachers the 'inspiration' of exciting ways of doing it. There are some good materials but generally they are too unimaginative for you to do more than 'dip into'. To get the best out of what is on offer, you have to adapt the materials to suit your needs. These Literacy Progress Units may be developed and improved as the years go by, but it is equally possible that they could wither on the vine along with the rest of the National Literacy Strategy. The phrase that is already being used to countenance this possible demise is 'beyond the National Literacy Strategy'. So, if you find good activities and exercises, you should squirrel them away for use in future years so that you are not taken by surprise.

Corrective reading schemes

There are a number of popular corrective reading schemes which you could consider using with struggling secondary school readers. I have chosen to focus on the ones I believe to be the most popular at present.

Accelerated Literacy Programme

This programme (Folens, 2001) describes itself as a 'second chance unit', so it is in many ways appealing to the same audience as the Literacy Progress Units. The programme is described as best taught in extra daily sessions for those who need extra support in basic understanding of the phonics and the word and syllable knowledge needed for reading and spelling.

The programme offers a very structured programme in which pupils read key words that conform to certain sound/letter patterns. Then they apply them to a series of sentences. The tight-knit structure of the programme makes it easy to pick up and use, and this feature would appeal to many learning support teachers and assistants. There is a lot of useful work in terms of reinforcing words and their meaning. But the drawback to the programme is that it is using disembodied sentences which just happen to fit in with the word patterns that the readers are supposed to be practising. So it is hard to build any sense of engagement with a sustained narrative, always a useful strategy with struggling older readers. As in the Progress Units, there are some good exercises to dip in and out of, but to build a whole reading recovery programme around such resources would be somewhat monotonous for many pupils.

The *Accelerated Literacy Programme* is available from Folens Publishers at Apex Business Centre, Boscombe Road, Dunstable LU5. There are seven units in the *Accelerated Literacy Programme*. Each unit currently costs £39.95 and the materials inside are photocopiable.

Toe by Toe

Toe by Toe: A Highly Structured Multi-sensory Reading Manual for Teachers and Parents by K. Cowling and H. Cowling is available from 8 Green Road, Baildon, West Yorkshire BD17 5HL. This is a fully fledged Phonics programme. The authors insist that every step must be followed and that all pupils, whatever their prior level of expertise, must start from the first exercise. The programme is designed for daily use, of up to twenty minutes and is tailored to suit one-to-one contact between the pupil and the adult, deemed the 'coach', who can be a teacher or a parent. According to *Toe by Toe*, parents have an advantage over teachers as they don't need to follow classroom routines and have a 'clean sheet'. However, in my experience, a teacher's relationship with the struggling reader is usually 'cleaner' than that of a parent, especially when it comes to working with their own offspring on reading. There is often a history of frustration and anger, which is very hard to overcome when youngsters have had years of failure.

Toe by Toe builds up letter sounds and letter/sound combinations and turns them into words and sentences. Pupils have to read them over a number of days to consolidate them. If they keep on getting a word wrong, then they must return to it until they are in need of no further 'coaching'. The sentences they are asked to read are designed to see whether they have secured their newly secured phonic skills and, according to the authors, are deliberately set up to prevent readers using 'context' to guess what the words say. Given that the use of context is one of the most important reading skills, this type of reading will inevitably switch some pupils off.

What are the good points of the *Toe by Toe* programme for secondary school pupils?

* It offers a highly structured phonics programme that is not sullied by lots of primary school illustrations that older children find patronising.
* It reassures many learning support teachers and assistants in that it is very clearly laid out and easy to follow.
* It offers sensible advice for marking struggling readers without knocking back their already low self-esteem. A tick means you've got the answer right and a dot (not a cross) means you have got to work on it further. This avoids the psychological downer of having charts covered in crosses.
* *Toe by Toe*'s structure and frequency of delivery create a situation where an older pupil has a great chance of building up a positive relationship with an adult, one to one. The step by step approach brings a lot of regular opportunities for success. Whether the pupil works well with

phonics or not, the good 'karma' that can come from a regular positive learning environment can make a major improvement to somebody's reading very quickly.

There are some limitations to the *Toe by Toe* programme:

- The publishers insist that it is used every day, and, whilst this is very useful, in a busy secondary school it is very hard to set up. The creators also insist that a word should be 'coached' until the reader gets it right. Day after day, week after week? If you were to follow this prescriptive approach to the letter, some pupils would become very demoralized.
- Despite the explicit advice of *Toe by Toe*, it might be better used by dipping in and out of it alongside some real book reading using the general strategies suggested in Chapters 2 and 3 above.
- *Toe by Toe* is very expensive. Each pupil book costs £25 and is not photocopiable.
- In its later sections *Toe by Toe* produces very difficult formal language that low-aged secondary readers will find hard to read but almost impossible to understand – for example, words such as 'solidified', 'sophistry' and 'philanthrophy'.

THRASS

A. Davies and D. Ritchie, *Teaching Handwriting Reading and Spelling Skills*. Materials available from THRASS (UK) Ltd, Units 1–3, Tarvin Sands, Barrow Lane, Tarvin, Chester CH3 8JF. This is a phonics-based scheme, which has a big presence in Australia, Europe and America. It has a catologue brimming with lots of reinforcing materials as well as the main programme file. This resource pack currently costs £100, but the promotional material hints that THRASS cannot be delivered without its teachers having extra training, which means that THRASS introduction can be expensive for a school.

THRASS sets out to teach the forty-four phonemes (speech sounds) in the English language and, from them, individual word reading. The creators of the scheme accept that it should be combined with a balanced literacy programme and that using it alone it is not a guaranteed panacea.

THRASS illustrations are a little on the 'young' side, passable for Year 7 but less motivating for Year 9 and over. However, its structured phonic approach will appeal to some secondary pupils with reading difficulties. The major limitation has already been considered in Chapter 3 when looking at phonic interventions. Many older pupils have already seriously turned off phonics and will disintegrate emotionally if they have their noses rubbed in phonemes and word level work, yet again. There are cheaper ways of making light-touch phonic interventions (see Chapter 3), but, if you can afford THRASS as well, it would be a useful resource to dip into.

Ruth Miskin's Literacy Programme for Secondary Schools

Ruth Miskin's Literacy Programme is being piloted in secondary schools at the time of writing this book. Advice and materials available by emailing her at rthmiskin@aol.com. It is aimed at Year 7 and 8. In many ways it offers the most carefully thought out and comprehensive way of addressing reading recovery in secondary schools within a structured-intervention model of working. The programme sets out, like many other corrective reading schemes, to teach the forty-four grapheme/phoneme correspondences in the English language. What makes the programme practical and appealing is that Ruth Miskin has combined phonics with opportunities for reading short stories to reinforce the sound/letter mapping skills the pupils have just learnt. Pupils also get the opportunity to complete written questions about the text, which helps them practise their comprehension skills. Each booklet also offers the opportunity of a more extended written response to the text with a simple writing frame. The pupils also practise the spelling of vocabulary that they are looking at. The Miskin programme allows pupils to work in pairs, which makes the lesson more varied and entertaining for them.

As always, the crunch point is whether the texts that Miskin has included are genuinely as lively and inviting as they claim to be. It is a tall order to create a story which is truly readable and also builds up patterns of grapheme/phoneme correspondence systematically. From what I can see, the Miskin materials are a brave attempt that work well some of the time but could do with some fine tuning. The only anecdotal feedback that I have obtained from one secondary school, Selhurst High School for Boys in Croydon, suggested that the scheme was generally working well but that many pupils with poor reading got tired of the routine chanting of the grapheme chart. The programme was being used in English lessons, and some of the teachers had cut back on doing it every lesson, that is to say one hour a day. They had gone back to more traditionally styled English lessons for at least three out of the five lessons a week to break a feeling of monotony created by the intensive Miskin routine.

The Miskin scheme's materials are reasonably priced but the training for teachers is expensive. However it looks like a interesting and more multi-dimensional approach to corrective reading at secondary school than anything else currently on the market. Like all the other corrective reading schemes, it has the clear advantage of giving learning support teachers or assistants a very clear framework to work to, which many will find very reassuring. The standard 'boredoms' created by the phonic-based approach lurk as always in the background.

Finding good commercial reading books

Low-aged readers and teachers at secondary level cannot live by corrective reading schemes alone. They need entertaining reading books that give them a real reason to read together. Literacy recovery pupils are like anybody else: they want reading material that will grip them. They often have a greater need for this than most other groups of readers because their mechanical reading skills are relatively weak. The last thing they need is reading material which is too difficult and boring or material which is too easy and patronizing.

Over the last four years I have been buying reading texts for low-aged secondary readers and feeling dissatisfied with what I've been getting. With a few exceptions, the books have promised a lot and ended up being disappointing. I have, like many Special Needs budget holders, made the fatal mistake of buying lots of booklets without actually reading them first. The golden rule of selecting texts for low-aged readers is to read them yourself. Most are less than 2500 words, and if you find them boring the majority of pupils will most likely agree with you. It's probably better to have eight copies of a good read for group use than eight single copies of different poor-quality readers.

The main pitfalls

There are general problems with the fiction readers for our target pupils. They always claim to be 'high-interest low-aged readers', but often the reality is that they are rather wooden and stilted. Many patronise the teenage reader, giving them subject matter which is beneath their level of sophistication. The fiction authors fail to create the most basic ingredients of an effective story, such as defining characters and creating a dramatic conflict between them. So 'Tim' or 'Sue' are just names on a page and simply ciphers for a series of actions to take place. The 'high-interest' readers end up in a series of monotonous actions where character names are interchangeable because they are so undeveloped. Many of the fiction readers fail to create a narrative with anywhere near the level of maturity of their teenage television and film counterparts. They don't use enough simple dialogue to develop characters and story lines like a good teenage television soap. Instead there is a concentration on reported action, which raises the reading age level of the texts and lowers the immediacy of the story line. There is often too much description alongside the reported action, which slows the narrative down and makes it more confusing to low-aged readers. The reading ages are usually higher than claimed in the advertising, and most books are also woefully short. A low-aged reader appreciates a decent length of story in the same way as anybody else. Despite some excellent front covers which can be very eye-catching, there are often only a few black and white illustrations inside to help the reader interpret the story.

The best of the readers

With some exception, the best readers are non-fiction texts, followed by the 'chillers' and 'horror' stories. The other reliable types of fiction texts are simplified versions of classic stories, retold. There are several excellent versions of Shakespeare's *Macbeth* and Dickens's *Great Expectations*. Their strength lies in the fact that they had good characterization and story lines to begin with.

Non-fiction provides the best range, with some excellent titles for both boys and girls. The books tend to be longer, and some have some excellent colour plates. The best won't go out of fashion but some will need replacing regularly, as books about pop stars and football teams date very quickly.

The main publishers for reluctant readers

Obviously, this section of the book will need periodic revision. However a lot of investment has gone into many of the series mentioned here and I think the publishers are more likely to develop than delete their brand names and titles. The reluctant reader field is one where there is a lot of money to be made.

Nelson Thornes

Nelson Thornes (www.nelsonthornes.com) has the *Zone 13* series, a collection of science fiction books. They are tales of the unexplained, and are suitable for some young secondary school readers. The *Spirals* have been going for twenty-five years and are a solid 'chiller thriller' series of titles with some good story lines. These are some of the best readers available as they are a reasonable length and make an effort to develop 'character' and dramatic tension. As a small-group reader you'll get a reasonable amount of reading time for your money out of most *Spirals*. There is also a series, entitled *Premier Fiction* readers. Their subject matter is largely too young for most readers aged eleven to fourteen for whom they are intended.

Collins

Collins (www.collinseducation.com) has several series of reading resources aimed at eleven-years-olds and over. The *Soundbites* series claims to be for the eleven to fourteen age range. Some of the non-fiction texts and the retold classics are excellent. There is a tendency to underestimate the reading ages, so many of the texts labelled as for ages eight or nine are more difficult than they claim to be.

Hodder and Stoughton Educational

Hodder (www.hodderheadline.co.uk) is the market leader in terms of the huge investment it has put into titles. Many of their books are approved with a Basic Skills kite mark, which has obviously enhanced their credibility with teachers. Many of the fiction titles have problems that have been outlined as general to this market niche. The *Live Wire Investigates* series has some very interesting general knowledge titles with something for everybody. There is everything from *Bungee Jumping* to *Being a Model* and *Hang Gliding* to *The Bermuda Triangle*. There are some fascinating titles in the *Live Wire Real Lives* section, although this is certainly an area where titles could date. Martin Luther King is probably always a safe bet, but is footballer Michael Owen? There are also series of plays, classics, chillers and sci-fi. Hodder *Live Wires* provide teachers' books with photocopiable worksheets and have some texts on tape.

However, our general criticisms of reluctant reader books applies here. *Live Wires* are usually sold in mixed packs and are quite expensive for what they are, especially if you end up selecting titles that don't work with your pupils. In some series the books have colour covers, but no pictures inside. The page lay-out is sometimes very strange, with short lines with hardly any words on them. This spoils the 'real book' feel that reluctant readers need as much as any other reader.

Heinemann

Heinemann (www.heinemann.co.uk) is also one of the big publishers in the reluctant reader field. They have a *High Impact* series of plays, fiction and non-fiction. As usual, the non-fiction stands out, with some interesting titles, such as *Once Bitten: The Story of Shark Attacks* and *Football Crazy* with offbeat tales that would suit fantasy footballers. *Special Effects in Film* and *Unsolved Mysteries* are expensive but have some excellent illustrations.

Folens Publishers

Folens (www.folens.com) has just developed an interesting-looking series of low-aged reading books called *On The Edge*, with soap-style teenage plots.

Assessment

Overall, the quality of low chronological reading age booklets for secondary schools is getting better. It's a pity the major publishers tend to duplicate each other's range of materials with very similar titles, rather than attempt to break new ground with less patronizing fiction that mirrors the best of what television youth culture has to offer. The range and variety of non-fiction texts is impressive. Much of the fiction remains anaemic and slightly patronizing. It won't impress teenagers of twelve, let alone of fifteen.

Many of the texts are very expensive when you consider the limited amount of classroom time it takes for even a slow reader to read one aloud to you. You can buy an English textbook with hours of literacy work for two or three pounds more than a low-aged reading booklet which occupies three lessons' worth of work at most!

Many publishers are also guilty of underestimating how difficult their texts are and often mislead by describing a book as having a reading age of eight to nine when it's at least two years higher. The golden rule must be: don't waste departmental money without reading the book yourself first, or, better still, reading it with pupils. Most companies give you between twenty and thirty days to inspect a copy. They seem to pack the books in such a way that, once opened, they are very hard to repack, so open them carefully. As one cynical head of department suggested, this could be a cunning sales ploy to get you to keep the books because it's simply too much hassle to send them back during a busy school day.

Assessing the suitability of reading material

Whether you are deciding to buy specialized material from the reluctant reader market or looking for a text in an English textbook, newspaper, magazine or school library, you need ways of assessing the suitability for your pupils. The best texts are going to be relevant to the personal experiences, knowledge, interests and level of maturity of your low-aged readers. This was one of the key principles for a successful literacy intervention established in Chapter 2.

You can run an MOT text on a piece of text, before using it. You don't have to draw out a table and test exhaustively for all the headings. It's enough to do a quick reconnaissance for your individual pupils as a mental exercise of a couple of minutes. Your three main considerations are:

- subject matter
- difficulty of the language
- difficulty of the text structure.

Subject matter

Does the text reflect experiences that will strike a chord in the pupil's knowledge of the world? Many of the so-called high-interest low-reading-age fiction series available commercially show a white middle-class world. They reflect the direct experience of significant numbers of their writers, many of whom have never worked in a secondary school, let alone one which has many pupils with low-level literacy. The same is almost certainly true for most of the commissioning editors who decide what will be published.

Our secondary low-aged readers need texts which are written in language that reflects their life experience or have such powerful universal human impact that they can transcend class and cultural barriers. Your job is to find the texts that get closest to this, and which are culturally inclusive. Unfortunately they tend to be scarce in the low-reading-age market.

Difficulty of the language

Many low-aged readers use an informal language world to express themselves. They flounder with certain kinds of more formal language and writing. It's worth scanning a new text for the following kind of pitfalls.

Connectives

Are ideas in the narrative joined together with connectives that will confuse weak readers and make it hard for them to follow the sense? For example, difficult linking words will confuse many of our readers:

- *Connectives that indicate cause and effect*: due to, as a result of, because of
- *Connectives that indicate comparison and contrast*: whereas, on the other hand
- *Connectives that indicate concession*: anyhow, nevertheless, in spite of.

Unfamiliar subject vocabulary

Is there much specialized subject vocabulary in the writing that will confuse pupils – for example in history, words such as 'vote', 'democracy', 'pressure group' and 'trend'.

Synonyms are often used to avoid repeating the same piece of subject vocabulary. But the substitute words can be less obvious to a poor reader. For example 'home' could become 'dwelling' and 'abode'. But many of our readers will stumble on the alternative words.

Difficulty of the text structure

Confusing pronouns

Are there problems around the subject and a linking pronoun? 'He', 'she', 'it' can all cause problems. I have found that many low-aged readers can confuse 'he' with 'she' when they begin to struggle with reading accurately and hold on to meaning.

Length of sentences

Long sentences with subordinate clauses will confuse the weak reader. Here is a typical example from a science textbook: 'If the computer's battery is charged on the second day and the position of the battery charger dial noted over the period of an hour, it will be observed that the machine gets warmer as the charge becomes full.'

Sentences with a large amount of description

Texts with much supporting description will cause weaker readers to falter. Yet many of the reluctant-reader booklets allow themselves to indulge in it, instead of using dialogue to convey the vital points of action and interaction.

Passive voice

The passive voice is often used in a piece of writing to convey a sense of objectivity in subjects such as science, geography and history. It can confuse low-aged readers. For example: 'The test tube was heated over a bunsen burner.'

Summary

These are some of the main questions you should ask yourself about any text for low-aged readers:

- Is it about a subject that pupils can tune into?
- Is there a lot of formal language in it?
- Is there a lot of specialist subject language in it?
- Will grammatical structures make it hard to read and understand? (The main problems are with connectives, pronouns, use of passive voice and long sentences with subordinate clauses or much description.
- Has this text got a lot of dialogue? Direct speech is almost always a strong selling point.

Writing your own texts with the pupil

One of the best ways of providing good resources to read with your pupils is to write them yourself.

Try writing a text in partnership with your pupil, on the spot, in a reading lesson. The pupil can speak and you can structure the story, sometimes simplifying what the pupil says into words that you know that they will have a good chance of being able to read back to you later; at other times keeping in some harder words so that they can expand their 'sight vocabulary'. Writing your own texts with the pupil is the best way of ensuring that a written passage has a theme of interest to your weak reader.

If you use a word processor or one of the simple pieces of software that allow you to create a simple story frame, you can give the pupils an even greater sense of ownership over the process of writing and reading back. (See Chapter 8.) The biggest advantage of a word processor is that it allows you to create printed texts that are easier to read. If you decide to handwrite a story, then you must make your handwriting sufficiently clear for it not to become another major impediment for a struggling reader.

Further reading

Durran, J. and Stewart, J. (2000) *Student Handbook for English* (Pearson). This book covers the same ground as the Progress Units, in a much simpler and more imaginative way. Perhaps it's better because it was written by two serving heads of English!

Chapter 6

Creating new materials

In this chapter we look at the ways we can help low-age secondary pupils cope with the reading and writing demands of the curriculum. Given that the average secondary school textbook has a reading age of twelve plus, such pupils are likely to be way out of their reading comfort zone most of the time. The main text will be too difficult and dense for them and they will not be able to read the 'activities sections', let alone look back in the text for the answers. This overriding problem gives learning support teachers two important tasks to perform regularly:

- finding ways of making an original text readable, at least in part, for the low-aged reader. This means creating shorter reading activities around the longer text that pick out the essence of that original text.
- changing the work activities so that the pupil can respond orally and in writing to the original text from the abridged reading experience they have had.

The technical term for finding ways of making difficult texts more accessible to individual pupils is 'differentiation'. Differentiation can be done in a variety of ways. Some involve careful oral questioning and others involve written activities that give the pupils the chance to rehearse what they understand and can do.

There follows a simple ten-point differentiation list for all teachers who work with struggling readers to attach to their teacher planners as an aide memoire for them each lesson. All the strategies can be done on the spot and adopted without preparation.

- Assume that any low-aged readers in the class will be unable to read your standard text. At reading ages of between eight and nine and a half they won't be able to access meaning.
- Write the key words for the lesson on the board. Explain them.
- Get the whole class to copy them down along with a simple definition. Set the agenda with the key learning points of your lesson.
- If you are going to use a text, explain what it is about in advance in simple language. What can the reader expect? This will help and reassure poor readers.
- Are there any pictures in the texts you are using? If so, ask for any open-ended questions about them. Pictures are very good way of getting everybody involved.
- When you want the class to do some writing, explain very clearly what you want them to do. Give the same clear and simple instructions again to pupils with literacy difficulties – individually, if you get the chance. Get them to repeat those instructions to you, using their own words.
- Write an example of what you would like to see the pupils writing. Put it on the board as a model that the whole class can copy.
- Sit a poor reader next to a good one. Allow some paired reading in the lesson. Make it explicit to the good reader that you want them to help their neighbour.
- Make up a simple cloze exercise (see examples in this chapter) about the key points of the lesson and put it on the board as the lesson draws to an end. Do it off the top of your head and get all pupils to complete it in the last five minutes. It will be especially helpful in reinforcing the main points of the lesson for struggling readers.

- The preceding points are very useful for pupils with low reading ages and general learning difficulties. But they are also good overall teaching strategies for everybody. The whole class will benefit.

DARTs activities

An essential way of opening up a difficult text to struggling readers is through a variety of strategies known as DARTs: Directed Activities Related to Texts. Their essential benefit is as an activity encouraging pupils into an interrogative approach to their reading – always something about which weak and reluctant readers feel very insecure.

The DARTs activities we are going to look at have certain common features that make them very useful for both learning support and mainstream teachers wishing to create materials for low-aged readers. They offer on-the-spot, instantaneous differentiation for one-to-one, small-group or whole-class situations. They can be created quickly in neat handwriting or typed on a portable computer. They can be written on a whiteboard or overhead projector. They are exercises which give your pupils a lot of writing to do, copying information but reorganizing it or adding to it as they go. This gives them the satisfaction of having a lot of written work on the page, and they won't feel as if they are falling seriously behind their class mates. Simple DARTs activities can be a lower-entry-level exercise that keeps some pupils learning purposefully, when other more highly literate pupils are engaged in more complex manipulations of the text appropriate to their competency level.

DARTs with photocopied text

You can create certain varieties of DARTs when you have photocopied text. Providing you don't mind using it just the once, you can let the pupils write on it. You can also delete parts of the text before you give it to the pupils. Both can help pupils develop their literacy skills.

Now read the story of *Werewolf Eclipse*. This book was designed for low-aged secondary readers between eleven and sixteen years old. It has an overall reading age of around nine and a half but the amount of dialogue makes it slightly easier. We will use this text to model some of the directed activities related to text.

Chapter One

Mexico City

Millions of people had come to the city to see the Eclipse. As the big shadow fell over the city, F.B.I. agents looked for the murderer. They knew he would be there. But would they get him before he killed again?

It was just three minutes to the total eclipse. Three minutes to when the sun passed behind the moon. Three minutes to when the day would become dark and silent. And there was a race against time which the agents lost. The murderer struck at five people in a back street. The victims died terrible deaths. They were torn apart. It was like an attack by a wild animal. One luck girl was badly bitten but she lived.

London – Vauxhall. Secret Service H.Q.

'Agent Parker – you are getting good at this,' Laura Turnbull said. They had been doing karate training for nearly one hour.

'Do you really think so?' he replied.

'We will finish with fifty sit ups,' she instructed.

'Fifty, are you trying to kill me, Laura?' he moaned.

One hour later they were having breakfast together.

'You seem a lot more relaxed since you started working out,' Turnbull said.

'I enjoy it because we are spending a lot of time together,' he replied.

'We are spending nearly twenty four hours a day together. I might as well share a bed with you,' she joked. Robert Parker looked like he had been stung by a bee. He changed the subject quickly. 'So do you think I have the makings of a killer?' he asked nervously.

'Not a chance Parker. But if you want to see a terrible killer. Come and read the details of this new Mexico case.'

They studied the photos of the victims.

'The patterns of killings are always the same. Each time there is a full eclipse of the sun, at the place of longest darkness. Mexico last year, Australia and Japan before that,' she explained.

'The victims are bitten and clawed. They have traces of dog hair on their skin,' Parker commented, looking at a picture. 'I am no expert, but it's possible that we have a werewolf on our hands.'

They were both silent.

'I was afraid you would say that,' she said.

'And we have a total eclipse in Cornwall in one week,' he added. He checked the computer. 'David Wood near St David will be the longest place of darkness. Three minutes and 25 seconds.'

'What can we do?' she asked.

'Fly Angela Lopez over from Mexico. The girl who was badly bitten but lived. According to the myth, werewolves don't like to leave unfinished business,' he said.

'You mean use a young frightened girl as bait,' Turnbull exclaimed. 'That's a terrible idea!'

'But we have to be there when the murderer strikes. It's the only way to save other peoples' lives. Besides Angela may be able to give us useful information,' he explained.

'But it says here that she can't remember anything,' Turnbull read.

'Her memory may come back when the eclipse of the sun begins,' he said. 'The werewolf will almost certainly be near then.'

'I don't like it,' Turnbull said, shivering.

'Nor do I, but it's our only chance.'

Chapter Two

They met Angela Lopez at the airport and took her to London.

She was happy to help them.

'We will be taking you down to St David's tomorrow,' Turnbull explained.

'You do know I can't remember anything about the attack. All I remember is waking up in hospital. Will that be enough?'

The Agents nodded sympathetically and left her to rest.

Parker made plans on his mobile phone. There was a lot to think about. Over two million people would be travelling to Cornwall to watch the Eclipse. They had to stop the murderer from hiding in the crowd.

'We will trap him in David Wood. He will want to get near Angela. If he's a werewolf, he will smell her blood,' Parker explained.

'You and your werewolves,' said Turnbull.

'Come on Agent Turnbull. Have you watched Angela. She is acting strangely.'

'She seems ok to me.'

'She is getting weaker. It's like the werewolf is sucking her blood.'

'Maybe she is just bored with your company,' Turnbull joked.

Parker ignored her.

'There are only 24 hours to go to the Eclipse. Let's hope she remembers something quickly. We really need some help,' he said.

On the evening before the Eclipse the two agents sat watching television with Angela. Suddenly she slumped in her chair. Her breathing had become shallow. Her face was covered in sweat.

'Angela, what's wrong?' shouted Turnbull.

'I feel shivers down my spine. It is like claws in my back,' she sobbed.

'Can you see him, Angela?' Parker asked.

She nodded weakly.

'Can you draw him for me?'

She nodded again.

They put her on the sofa. They covered her with a blanket. She drew very quickly onto the computer paper. Parker grabbed it.

'I'll be back in a second Angela,' he promised. Turnbull stayed with her and held her hand. Parker rushed into the other room. He fed the paper into his lap-top computer. 'I don't believe it, I don't believe it. It can't be true,' he muttered to himself. 'Turnbull, come and look at this.'

She ran in. 'What is it?'

'Look carefully,' he said, pointing at the screen.

'It looks like a picture of a dog to me,' she remarked.

'A werewolf,' he corrected her.

'I had worked that out stupid.'

'But look at its face?' he pressed.

'I don't get you.'

'Look properly.'

'Alright, alright, give me a chance,' she replied.

'What do you see?'

'I told you – a shaggy dog.'

He clicked a button on his computer. 'Now what do you see?'

'Oh no, no,' she moaned. 'It can't be.'

'It's Angela Lopez,' he whispered.

They heard a window smashing. They ran into the sitting room. But Angela had jumped out into the night.

Chapter Three

Parker got on the phone to all police units.

'Security alert. Murder suspect is Angela Lopez. She is dressed in a blue shirt and black trousers when last seen. She will look very strange. She has hair all over her face and very long teeth. Do not approach. She is very dangerous!'

Angela ran through David Wood. She was howling like a wolf. She seemed to be in pain. Her arms and legs were getting longer. Her face was growing hair. She was becoming a Werewolf! Parker sat with his head in his hands. He was feeling shocked. 'I should have guessed. A person who has been attacked by a werewolf and not killed, becomes one.'

'It wasn't your fault,' Turnbull said.

Parker looked at his watch and then at the sky. 'The sun is moving behind the moon. It's beginning,' he whispered. They pushed through the crowds of people, standing on every pavement. Parker's mobile rang.

'Angela Lopez has been seen in David Wood,' he shouted. 'We've got her. The wood is blocked off.'

They ran towards it. When they got there, the Eclipse was starting. The sky darkened suddenly. The flowers were closing up. The birds had stopped singing.

'Let us through,' Turnbull shouted.

'Nobody is allowed,' said the Policeman.

'So what are those two doing?' screamed Parker. He pointed to a young woman and a child in a push chair.

'Oh, I said they could use the loo. The kid needs a nappy change.'

They pushed past him and ran towards the toilets. It was completely dark now.

'Get out of there,' screamed Turnbull.

They dragged them away from the wash basins. The child started to cry.

Suddenly they heard a wolf's howl. A huge beast leapt out at them. It ripped the cover off the push chair with its teeth. Turnbull scissor kicked it in the back. The werewolf turned on her. It snapped at her face. One shot fired out and the werewolf fell down. There was the sound of screaming and panic.

The Police ran towards them with torches. But the sun passed from behind the moon. Daylight returned. The Eclipse was over.

The werewolf was dead. They stood watching it slowly turning back into Angela Lopez. Parker was grief stricken when he saw her. He began to sob. Turnbull comforted him. The Police took mother and child away.

Chapter Four

Turnbull and Parker went back in their office two days later.

'So have they been checked out?' he said.

'I heard Commander Watson say the mother is fine. The girl has a cut on her arm.'

'A cut?' Parker asked nervously.

'Could be a bite. Could be a scratch. They are not going to take any chances,' she explained.

'What does that mean exactly?' he demanded.

'It means they are going to kill the child,' she said in a whisper.

'Because of what it might become. That's terrible!' he shouted.

'The Commander said it would be top secret. There will be an accident. Mum will never know.'

'Oh that makes it alright then. When will they do it?' Parker demanded.

'Tomorrow night,' Turnbull whispered.

Parker knew what he had to do. He went to the hospital.

He got past the police guards using his I.D. He found Rosie. He carried her away in a blanket and drove her home.

'What's my darling little Rosie doing here? The hospital told me that they still had tests to do' said her Mum.

Parker spoke in a low voice. He had covered his face with a handkerchief. 'Take her. Don't ask any questions. Get away from here and never come back.'

'But........' Mum replied.

'No "buts"! Rosie's life is in danger. Just take her away. Don't ask me who I am. Just think of me as her fairy godmother."

He passed the child over quickly and disappeared.

When he got back, Turnbull was waiting for him. 'I know what you have done,' she said.

'You do?' he replied.

'I don't blame you. Every human being has the right to life.'

Parker nodded. 'I hope I did the right thing. I could not let them kill a child. She looked so sweet and innocent. If the Commander works out what I did, I am finished!'

'You were with me all day and you never went out of my sight,' Turnbull said, squeezing his arm.

Young Rosie had her second birthday a few days later. Agent Parker and Turnbull were not there to see her on this happy day. She was toddling across the garden. The family dog came up to her and wagged its tail. It sniffed her and howled. The hair on its back stood up and it ran out of the room.

Activities based on highlighting text

With a text such as this in photocopy, you can ask the pupils to look for certain linguistic features in the text – for example, underlining all the verbs or linking words on the first page. As a higher-level exercise, you can ask the pupils to rub out three words in Chapter Two of *Werewolf Eclipse*. They can be asked to select verbs. When this is done, they pass the amended script to the person next to them. The teacher asks the pupils to come up with an alternative action word for each empty space.

Highlighting can also be used to pick out conversation in the narrative. In Chapter One you could ask them to circle in one colour all the places where Laura Turnbull speaks and Robert Parker in another.

Text marking can also be used to pick out aspects of the 'action' in the narrative. Pupils can be asked to underline all the things that Angela was doing in Chapter Two.

Text can be marked for its descriptive dimension. Pupils can be asked to read Chapter Three and underline all the sentences and phrases that describe the atmosphere in the woods. This may include the sights and the sounds there.

Marking text can get pupils to focus on the overall meaning of a section of text. An exercise that would do this is asking readers to a title to give each of the chapters in *Werewolf Eclipse*. Then ask them to say why they have chosen their titles.

Advantages of these activities:

*   These are simple ways for you to involve the pupils with the text, without getting them to write very much.
*   They can be used in varied ways. Some activities explore the technical structure of the text and others explore the meaning of it and the way language is used.
*   You can focus the pupils on an explicit aspect of the text very quickly.
*   The above types of activities lend themselves to pair or group work, so the strong can support the weak.

Possible drawbacks:

*   It costs a lot of photocopying money to let pupils highlight copies of text, especially longer ones. It's hard to use them again when they are marked heavily.
*   There are copyright issues around photocopying significant slices of text.

DARTs with the original text

In this situation, highlighting is not an option. You can't mark the original and you can't use Tippex on it because it's a resource that has to be used again and again. It may be an expensive publication of which you just about have enough class copies. You can attempt a certain amount of text highlighting if you have sticky labels or 'post it' notes, which you can write on without defacing the original text.

However, there is still a lot you can still do with non-photocopiable original text to enrich understanding through a variety of differentiated written activities. Again we will refer to *Werewolf Eclipse* and use it as an example to demonstrate certain useful techniques of simplifying the text to capture its overall meaning.

Rewriting in simpler language

The literacy teacher can model an example of how a short section of the text can be written in a simpler, shorter way. If we use Chapter Two of *Werewolf Eclipse*, we can summarize the narrative in simpler language:

> Parker and Turnbull take Angela Lopez home from the airport. They hoped that the werewolf would smell her blood and come looking for her.

Using a flow diagram

You can show pupils how to summarize short pieces of information in the form of a flow diagram, as with the information in the first part of Chapter Three.

> Parker phoned the police units.
> ↓
> He warned them that Angela was turning into a werewolf.
> ↓

Parker thought he should have guessed that Angela was a werewolf. Turnbull told Parker that it wasn't his fault.

↓

Parker went into David Wood to look for Angela.

Using a spider diagram

You can use a spider diagram to show aspects of the story. For example, the pupils could be asked to construct a spider diagram based around words that describe Turnbull's personality during the whole of the story. The easiest way of doing this would be to give them a list of phrases from which they have to choose the correct ones:

- likes computers
- is a karate expert
- likes joking a lot
- always brave
- never supports her partner

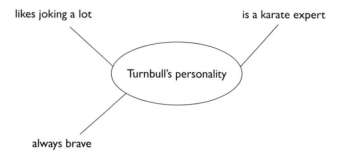

DARTs activities around comprehension

DARTs can be used regularly to test the pupils' understanding of a narrative.

Prediction

Predicting what is going to happen next in any narrative is an excellent way to assess how much a pupil understands about what has happened already. *Werewolf Eclipse* particularly lends itself to this kind of exercise because it concludes with an unresolved situation. Is the little girl Rosie going to grow up into a werewolf? The pupils could be asked to say how they think the story could continue. This could be written up with the title *Werewolf Eclipse Part 2*. Many fiction and non-fiction texts would benefit from having a prediction exercise built around them.

Cloze exercises

This is the most popular and regularly used DARTs activity. Very simple short texts can have cloze exercises around the whole of their content. As a text gets longer and more difficult, the low-aged reader is best focused on a short passage in the text of maybe a half page or a paragraph.

In the case of *Werewolf Eclipse* I have constructed a cloze exercise around the information in Chapter One. This is the kind of thing you can make up on the spot.

> The murders took place when there was an _____ of the sun. Parker and Turnbull knew that one person had survived the werewolf's attack in _____. Her name was _____ _____.

> Missing words (Lopez, eclipse, Mexico, Angela)

You can make a cloze exercise slightly more difficult by giving the first letter of the missing word but not a list of the missing words themselves.

> The murders took place when there was an e_____ of the sun. Parker and Turnbull knew that one person had survived the werewolf attack in M_____. Her name was A_____ L_____.

Or you can create a cloze exercise where you don't give missing words or first-letter clue.

Advantages of using cloze:

- It's a great way to get low-aged readers into a difficult text – and a useful warm-up or summary exercise for the whole class.
- Cloze exercises are very flexible, and can be short or long. Obviously, if you want to use them as a form of on-the-spot differentiation, then you are going to need to be able to write a relatively short passage quickly and give it a brief list of missing words.
- Cloze exercises give the pupils the maximum amount to write. In copying down the passage they are effectively writing out both question and answer. Having a lot to write can settle pupils down at turbulent times in the lesson.
- It gives the weaker literacy students a chance to write something that they are likely to get right. There will be a substantial amount of work in their exercise books.
- It avoids the 'copying' out of the textbook syndrome, which is also a low level exercise, so low on cognition that it's often a complete waste of time.

Possible drawbacks:

- Don't make them too long, as they can get confusing. (We look at an example of bad practice on p. 65 in an exercise based around a Key Stage Three history textbook.)
- Don't make them too long, as they need a lot of preparation.

True or false exercises

True or false exercises are another excellent form of on-the-spot differentiation. Like cloze, they help pupils show what they have understood from a difficult text, without setting a difficult series of open-ended questions that require independent writing in response. The pupils are given a series of statements as sentences. They are asked to copy out the ones that are true. Here is a simple example from *Werewolf Eclipse*:

> Robert Turnbull was the name of the male detective.
> **True or false?**
> The two agents had their headquarters at Vauxhall in London.
> **True or false?**
>
> The baby was bitten by the werewolf.
> **True or false?**
> Angela jumped out of the window. She had started to turn into a werewolf.
> **True or false?**

You can vary the pattern of true or false exercises by asking your pupils to write out the false statements as well, correcting them so that they become true.

Another variation is to create positive and negative statement pairs. The pupils read them and write out the correct one. For example:

> There was nobody in the toilets in David Wood.
> There was a mother and her baby in the toilets in David Wood.
>
> Parker was pleased with the way the Secret Service looked after the baby in hospital.
> Parker was furious to hear that the Secret Service intended to kill the baby in hospital.

Good points:

- As with cloze exercises, every word the teacher writes on the board or on a sheet is also written by the pupil. So it's easy to get a substantial amount of writing out of the pupil.
- As you can write a short true or false exercise quickly, you don't have to take your eye off a group of individuals or a whole class for long.
- It's the kind of differentiation that you can think of on the spot. But you can prepare it in advance and make it more elaborate if you've got time.
- Long true or false exercises can still work without becoming too confusing for a pupil with weak literacy skills. The same is not true for a long cloze exercise or sequencing exercises (see p. 62).

There are also drawbacks. Firstly, don't make the statements too similar to each other, with only a nuance of a difference between them. This will confuse low-aged readers. Here is an example from *Werewolf Eclipse*:

> Turnbull defended herself by kicking the werewolf.
> Turnbull defended the young child by scissor-kicking the werewolf in the back.

Compare this pair of statements with the earlier exercise. In the Parker statements we have clear and contrasting alternatives about what the Secret Service intended to do with the baby. Low-aged readers will find it easy to distinguish. However, the two Turnbull statements cover the same event in very similar ways. They are much harder to distinguish unless the reader pays careful attention to every detail. In the end it's clear than one is more detailed than the other and for that reason is most accurate of the statements. But low-aged readers would be confused by a nuance like this.

Secondly, your target group of students are likely to be better at saying yes or no to a factual statement than at dealing with one that requires inference from the text. For example:

> Parker was embarrassed by the way Turnbull teased him.
> Parker felt guilty for not guessing Angela Lopez was already a werewolf.

Both these statements require reading between the lines. They are much more difficult than a statement such as:

> Parker worked for the British Secret Service.

Matching half-sentences and writing them out

This is another easy way to produce on-the-spot differentiation to assess a low-aged reader's understanding of a text.

Here is short example of this kind of exercise from Chapter Three of *Werewolf Eclipse*. The pupils have to read the first halves of the sentences and must find the matching second halves before writing them out as full sentences:

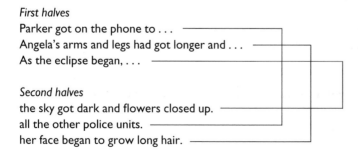

First halves
Parker got on the phone to . . .
Angela's arms and legs had got longer and . . .
As the eclipse began, . . .

Second halves
the sky got dark and flowers closed up.
all the other police units.
her face began to grow long hair.

Advantages:

- This technique is another type of differentiation around text that you can make up on the spot.
- Texts can be written on a board or overhead projector in a couple of minutes.
- Every word you write will need writing down and reorganization by the pupils, so it's time-effective.
- If you write the exercise into a pupil's exercise book or type it on to a sheet, the pupils can begin by joining the first and second halves of the sentences with arrows. (See p. 61.)

Drawbacks:

- If you make the exercise too long, pupils with poor reading skills will get confused by the sheer number of possible second-half alternatives.
- Splitting up the sentences can become messy in terms of lay-out. They can't be written up on a whiteboard or overhead projector as quickly as a true or false exercise.
- The joins between the first half and second half of the sentence have to work neatly. This makes it harder to think them out on the spot.

Sequencing exercises

In sequencing exercises the pupils are asked to put the sentences in the order in which they happen during the story. Here is a simple example from *Werewolf Eclipse*:

1 When they arrived in Cornwall, Angela started to feel weak and ill.
2 Angela Lopez was bitten by the werewolf in Mexico but she didn't die.
3 Suddenly she jumped out of the window and ran into David Wood.
4 Agents Parker and Turnbull brought her to London to see if she could give them any clues about the werewolf.
5 She began to turn into the werewolf.

Answers in order: 2, 4, 1, 3, 5.

Advantages:

- Everything you write gets used by the pupils, after they have reorganized it.
- This is often a higher level of cognitive exercise than true or false or cloze.

Drawbacks:

- Long sequencing exercises which explore fine detail and nuance in a narrative are very confusing. (See later sequencing exercise on pp. 66–69.)

Dialogue

Writing out a dialogue and finding out which characters say it is another good technique to differentiate a text and encourage pupils to follow the narrative. Here is a simple exercise from *Werewolf Eclipse*.

Ask your pupils to read Chapter One of the story. The pupils are forced to focus on a relatively short piece of text and look carefully at the conversations between the two characters in one particular scene. To give the pupils confidence, start off with a nice easy one. Was it Laura Turnbull or Robert Parker who said these things?

'Agent Parker – you are getting good at this.'

'Fly Angela Lopez over from Mexico. The girl who was badly bitten but lived.'

'But it says here that she can't remember anything.'

'I don't like it.'

Word squares

You can use word squares to test a pupil's understanding of a passage of writing. They can be set up like a mini-crossword puzzle. Here is an example from *Werewolf Eclipse*:

Ask the pupils to read the first twelve lines of Chapter One. Then fill in the word squares.

The agents have their headquarters there.

V			X		L	L

Being attacked by a werewolf was like being attacked by one.

W		D				M	L

The two agents finished their exercise routine with them.

S	I				

Answers: Vauxhall, wild animal, sit ups.

Tips:

- You make them easier if you give the first letter of the missing words.
- You make them easier if you set clues based on short sections of text.

Tips on all the above techniques

It's usually best to create them so that they cover only small parts of complicated text. This means that a pupil does not have to look too far to get the information. In case of sequencing, cloze and matching half sentences, don't make the exercise too long and detailed. This will put pupils under a lot of pressure. As always, variety is the best thing. Mix up the types of DARTs activities you use all the time. This will keep the pupils entertained and on their toes.

Drawing pictures and labelling them

Drawing pictures yourself and labelling them with short statements about the topic you are doing is another useful differentiation technique. If you can draw, you've got a very real and exploitable talent. Use visuals as a simple entry to a topic or a text. I have seen a history teacher use drawing skills to do a quick quirky caricature drawing of how Hitler stereotyped Jews. This was a great way into more text about the Nazi attitude towards Jews.

If you aren't good at drawing, then get a pupil to draw for you. Classes find it entertaining to see you or one of their classmates drawing. It rivets their attention and gets them into the topic you're learning about. We will be looking at ways of exploiting visual information in the next section of this chapter when we look at some good and bad examples of some of these differentiation techniques, using extracts from some popular National Curriculum textbooks.

Cloze exercises

PRIVATE LIVES

◆◆◆◆◆◆◆◆◆◆◆◆◆◆◆◆◆◆◆◆◆◆◆◆◆◆◆◆◆◆

Being married

> At the beginning of the sixteenth century husband and wife did not have a loving relationship. They spent little time together. Husbands were masters over their wives and had little affection for them. The main purpose of wives was to produce male heirs.
> By the eighteenth century husbands and wives were more affectionate and loved each other more. They were also more equal and spent more time together.

One problem we have in finding out about marriages in this period is that although just over half the population was female we know little about what women thought and felt. Much of our evidence about what women were like and about relationships between husbands and wives comes from the husbands!

Men believed that they were best at making decisions, at action and business, while women were meant to be maternal, domestic and obedient. Married women had few rights — as soon as they got married everything they owned became their husband's. A husband had the right to beat his wife, as long as the stick was no thicker than a man's thumb.

SOURCE 10 A scold's bridle. This was used as a punishment for nagging wives in the sixteenth century

> **1.** Look at Source 10. How do you think the scold's bridle worked?

SOURCE 11 Men's views of women
a) An extract from a sermon Bishop Aylmer gave to Queen Elizabeth

> *Women are of two sorts: some of them are wiser, better learned and more constant than a number of men, but some are foolish, wanton, flibbergibs, tattlers, witless, feeble, proud, dainty, tale-bearers, rumour-raisers and in everyway doltified with the dregs of the devil's dunghill.*

b) Extracts from the Homily on Marriage. This had to be read in church every Sunday from 1562

> *Woman is the weaker vessel, of a frail heart, inconstant, and with a word soon stirred to anger.*

> **2.** What do you think these terms from Source 11 mean: flibbergibs, tattlers?
> **3.** If you were a man in this period how would you use Source 11 to explain why you had the right to be in charge of your wife?

But were marriages really like this, with the wife doing as she was told all the time? Let's look at two marriages from the seventeenth century.

SOURCE 12 Extracts from the diary of Samuel Pepys

> *2 May 1663 I slept till almost 7 o'clock. So up and to my office (having had some angry words with my wife about her neglecting to keep the house clean, I calling her a 'beggar' and she calling me a 'prick-louse'). Returned home to dinner. Very merry and well pleased with my wife.*
> *19 December 1664 I was very angry and began to find fault with my wife for not commanding the servants as she ought. She gave me an angry answer. I did strike her over her left eye such a blow, as the poor wretch did cry out. But her spirit was such that she scratched and bit me.*
> *12 July 1667 . . . And so home, and there finding my wife in a bad mood for my not dining at home, I did give her a pull by the nose. I decided to go back to the office to avoid further anger. She followed me in a devilish manner, so I got her into the garden out of hearing (to avoid shame) and managed to calm her. Then I walked with her in the garden, and so to supper, pretty good friends, and so to bed.*

The first example (p. 64) is from *The Making of the UK* by Colin Shephard and Tim Lomas (John Murray, 1995). This is a popular history textbook for Key Stage Three, written by the creators of the innovative Schools History Project. It's a staple product in most secondary schools up and down the country and is typical of a history textbook in that it uses a number of historical source materials. The reading age of the book is at least twelve, which is in keeping with the Year 8 to 9 audience. So the text is beyond the fluency range of low-aged readers with reading scores between eight and ten years.

It's important to develop your eye for looking quickly at resources. If you withdraw groups or work in class using mainstream teaching materials, you'll need to adapt swiftly from one subject to another. Sometimes you will be able to plan in advance when a mainstream teacher can give you resources ahead of time. But the reality of most secondary classrooms is that you'll often have to cast your eye over the material on the spot and differentiate it there and then.

In its original form, page 18 is colour-coded. Source materials are in green and the basic narrative is in white, with the questions in yellow. There is a cartoon and a black and white source. It is this picture of a wife being punished by her nagging husband that represents the best way into this text. Talking about a picture and what it shows can act as a great 'ice-breaker'.

Further examination of the writing shows that Source 12 has a more straightforward narrative than Source 11. The main narrative in white has difficult words such as 'population', 'relationship', 'domestic', 'maternal' and 'obedient'. The cartoon summarizes the messages of the text.

Let's eliminate approaches to dealing with this page of Year 8 history.

Only the first of the three questions on the page is easily accessible to low-aged readers. The second requires a close analysis of the difficult Source 11, and the third needs sophisticated manipulation of Source 11.

However, we could make up some simpler DARTs activities to help access the text.

Good example

Pick a very short piece of the text to base a cloze exercise on – for example, a cloze based around the writing in the cartoon bubble 'Being married'. It needs to be short enough for us to write it quickly, with only a few missing words.

> At the beginning of the _____ century, husbands and wives did not have _____ relationships. Husbands were _____ over their wives. The main purpose of wives was to produce male _____.

(Missing words: heirs, sixteenth, loving, master)

Answers: sixteenth, loving, master, heirs.

Bad example

The following cloze is too long and detailed. It's spread out thinly across too much text. The number of words in the missing box will confuse low-aged readers.

> At the beginning of the sixteenth _____, husbands and wives did not have loving _____. We got all our evidence of this from the _____ themselves. Men believed they were the best at making _____. Women were meant to be _____ and _____.
>
> Women didn't have many rights so husbands were allowed to _____ them. If a wife nagged her husband she had to wear a _____ _____.
>
> Not all wives were as obedient as they should be. Source _____ is from the diary of Samuel Pepys. He explained that when he told his wife off she replied with an _____ answer. He hit her and she _____ and _____ him.

(missing words: century, bit, bridle, decisions, angry, scold's, men, obedient, maternal, relationships, beat, twelve, scratched)

Answers: century, relationships, men, decisions, obedient, maternal, beat, scold's bridle, twelve, angry, bit, scratched.

Sequencing exercises

This example is from *Buddhism* by Sue Penney in the Discovering Religions series (Heinemann, 1988). This is a staple book in religious studies departments. We will look at a good example of a regularly used DARTs exercise in the form of sequencing, followed by an example inappropriate for low-aged readers.

Pages 8–9 of this textbook (pp. 67–8) introduces the life of the Buddha, Siddattha Gotama. It looks at his life as a young prince and then begins to examine his search for enlightenment.

The chapter ends with a series of questions on p. 9. Almost all of them require the reader to look carefully over the two pages of the text. Only the three simple questions of the 'Test yourself' section on p. 9 are accessible to low-aged readers. They refer to a small box of text immediately above them and to a simple answer from the beginning of p. 8.

So the learning support teacher needs to create a written activity which allows much greater accessibility to text than the publisher is providing here for mainstream school readers.

Sequencing: a good example

You can create a simple sequencing exercise around Siddattha's early life:

1 **On his ride**, he saw an old man, a sick man, a dead man and a holy man. His new experience made him want to change his life.

2 **When** he was sixteen, he married a beautiful girl and they lived in a beautiful palace. He seemed to have everything he wanted.

3 Siddattha was born at Lumbini in Nepal.

4 **But despite all this**, Siddattha got bored and decided he would ride out of the palace grounds to see the world property.

Answers: 3, 2, 4, 1.

Good points:

- The information to complete it comes from just three paragraphs of the text under one heading in the book, 'Siddattha's early life'.
- It limits the chronological sequencing to big sweeps rather than small details.
- It keeps the sequence relatively short. It's easier to get four rather than eight information chunks in the correct order.
- It tries to make it easier for the reader by providing natural language links in the sequenced sentences. So one thing joins easily to the next. Examples of helpful 'connectives' are shown in **bold**.

The life of the Buddha

This section tells you about the life of Siddattha Gotama, the Buddha.

Siddattha's early life

Siddattha Gotama was an Indian prince. He was born at Lumbini, in what is today called Nepal, in the fifth century BCE. The stories say that when Siddattha was born, his father asked eight wise men what he would become. All of them agreed that he would be a great man, but they said that if he ever saw suffering, he would become a great religious leader rather than a great ruler. Siddattha's father ordered that no one who was sick or old should be allowed near the prince. Siddattha grew up to be handsome and clever. When he was sixteen he married a beautiful girl, and they had a son. Siddattha was rich and powerful – it seemed that he had everything he could want.

However, Siddattha became bored with his sheltered life in the palace, and one day he went riding outside the palace grounds. While he was out, four things disturbed him very much. He saw an old man – he had never seen old age before. He saw a sick man – he had never seen illness before. He saw a funeral, with the relatives weeping around the body. He had never seen sorrow or death before. As he was thinking about these things, he saw a holy man. The man was contented and happy, and said that he had given up his home and his family to wander from place to place searching for the answers to the problem of suffering in the world.

Siddattha was deeply disturbed by what he had seen, and decided that he, too, must try to find the answer to this problem. He left the palace that night, changed his royal robes for the simple clothes worn by holy men, and shaved his head.

Siddattha's search for Enlightenment

For the next six years, Siddattha travelled around India. He spent some time with two great teachers, then with a group of **monks**. He spent several years with five holy men who lived a very hard life, eating and drinking almost nothing. The idea was that if you force your body to suffer, it becomes less important to you. He found that starving himself did not help him to find any answers, so he began eating and drinking again. The holy men left

This old painting shows Siddattha leaving his palace

8

The Mahabodhi temple at Bodh Gaya

him in disgust, because they thought he had given up. Siddattha travelled on until at last he came to a great tree. Today this is called the **bodhi tree**, which means 'tree of wisdom'. He sat under the tree and meditated, and at last he gained Enlightenment. In other words, he achieved understanding of the meaning of life. Buddhists say that this is a feeling of total peace, when you can stop thinking about yourself and become totally free.

From this time on, Siddattha Gotama was called 'the Buddha'. According to Buddhist teaching, having achieved Enlightenment, Siddattha could have left Earth, but he chose not to do this. He believed that his knowledge should be passed on to others, so he spent the rest of his life teaching other people about the right ways to live. He passed away (Buddhists do not say that he died) at the age of 80. His body was **cremated**, and the ashes were placed in special burial mounds called **stupas**. Buddhists say that the Buddha's passing away was when he entered **Parinirvana**. This is the name given to the 'complete' Nirvana at the end of a Buddha's life.

PEOPLE

New words

Bodhi tree the 'tree of wisdom' under which the Buddha achieved Enlightenment
Cremate burn a body after death
Monk man who dedicates his life to his religion
Parinirvana complete Nirvana
Stupa place where part of the Buddha's ashes were buried

Test yourself

Where was Siddattha born?

What's a monk?

What's Parinirvana?

Things to do

1 What were the four things which Siddattha saw outside the palace? Why did they disturb him so much?

2 Explain why the monks lived such a hard life. Why do you think they were so disgusted with Siddattha when he gave up their way of living?

3 How could meditation help Siddattha to find the answer to the meaning of life?

4 Draw a series of pictures to show important events in the life of Siddattha Gotama. Use these words as titles: Prince, Meeting suffering, Meditating, Teaching.

9

Sequencing: a bad example

Now a sequencing exercise from the same section of the text which is likely to confuse low-aged readers.

1   He stayed with two great teachers.
2   Siddattha was an Indian Prince.
3   Siddattha was born in Nepal.
4   He was so disturbed by what he saw, he got out of his royal robes and changed into pauper's clothes.
5   Eight wise men said Siddattha would become a great man.
6   Siddattha became bored by his sheltered life in the palace.
7   He went out riding and saw lots of different types of people.
8   He travelled around India for six years.
9   Then he stayed with a group of monks.

Answers: 2, 3, 5, 6, 7, 4, 8, 1, 9.

Bad points:

*   There are nine parts to the sequence. Anything so long and detailed is hard to get into the right order.
*   To get the sequencing correct requires analysis of the whole text on p. 8, not just one carefully highlighted section.
*   The exercise repeatedly uses 'Siddattha' and 'He', which makes it hard to distinguish sequential development through connecting words.
*   The only way to do this kind of sequence properly is to refer very closely to the order in the text. Lower-aged readers find this kind of close cross-referencing very difficult.

True or false exercises

The third example is from Key Stage Three Geography text *Foundations*, by David Waugh and Tony Bushell (Stanley Thornes, 1996). This is one of the most popular geography textbooks of the last ten years, first published in 1991 and recently revised. It's part of a series that has an extra pack of resources for slow learners. But despite the availability of good SEN materials, you will often find yourself in classrooms where only the main textbook is in use. So you need the vital skills to differentiate on the spot. The book is well laid out and has excellent colour diagrams and photographs. These are always a good way into the text.

Page 38 is a section on how fresh water is obtained. It has two diagrams to use as a lead-in. The text is divided neatly into three sections, each with a leading question. We will use this extract (p. 70) to model some good and bad examples of true or false exercises and either/or sentences, a variation on the true or false theme.

Good example

Good true or false exercises should:

*   use a clearly defined piece of text
*   use the information from any simple graphics
*   give clear contrasting statements.

This true or false exercise is based on the pie chart and the numbered points about getting reliable fresh water in Britain:

3 River basins

How can supplies of fresh water be obtained?

What are the main sources of fresh water?

With over three-quarters of the earth covered in water there should be plenty for plants, animals and people. Unfortunately over 97 per cent of that water is in the seas and oceans (diagram **A**). As this is salt water it cannot be used by life on land. To make matters worse, three-quarters of the fresh water is held in storage as ice or snow (diagram **A**). This water can only become available if the world's glaciers and icecaps melt.

How do we get reliable supplies of fresh water in Britain?

Diagram **B** shows five main ways. These are listed below.

1 Most of the available fresh water is stored underground in rocks. It may be obtained by sinking wells and boreholes.

2 Sometimes underground water flows naturally out of a hillside as a spring.

3 Rivers would appear to be an obvious source of water. Unfortunately many are polluted and water from them has to be cleaned before it can be used.

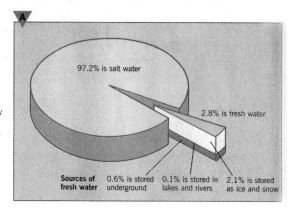

97.2% is salt water

2.8% is fresh water

Sources of fresh water   0.6% is stored underground   0.1% is stored in lakes and rivers   2.1% is stored as ice and snow

4 Lakes form natural stores of water on the earth's surface. Water from them may be sent (transferred) to large cities by aqueducts and pipes.

5 Dams are built to hold back rivers and to form artificial lakes called reservoirs. Water is released from reservoirs at a steady rate. The river channel is used to transfer water, replacing the old method of aqueducts and pipes.

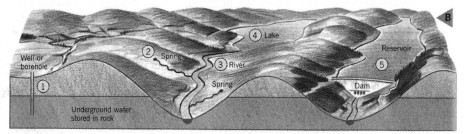

Well or borehole ①
② Spring
③ River
④ Lake
Spring
Reservoir
Dam
⑤
Underground water stored in rock

How is water transferred from one area to another?

Although in Britain we get far more rain than we need, it does not always fall where it is needed. Diagram **C** and the rainfall map on page 21 show that most rain (the **supply**) falls in the mountainous parts of north and west Britain where fewer people live. The biggest need (the **demand**) is in the flatter south and east where most people live. Therefore water is stored in those areas with the largest supply and transferred to those areas with the biggest demand.

Look at the pie chart. Now write out the statements that are true.

1 The percentage of water that is salt water is 50 per cent. *True or false?*

2 0.6 per cent of water is stored underground. *True or false?*

3 2.8 per cent of water is fresh. *True or false?*

Now look at the section, 'How do we get reliable supplies of fresh water in Britain?'

Choose the correct sentence from the pair of sentences and write it out.

EITHER
1 Most fresh water is stored underground in rocks.
OR
2 Most fresh water is stored in ponds.

EITHER
1 Rivers are always a good source of clear water.
OR
2 Rivers are often so polluted that the water has to be cleaned before it is used.

EITHER
1 Dams are built to hold back rivers and to create artificial lakes called reservoirs.
OR
2 Dams are built to clean dirty water.

Answers: False, true, true; 1, 2, 1.

Good points of the sentence pairing:

- They are very contrasting statements.
- They are taken from a very small and clearly defined part of the text.

Bad example

Bad true or false exercises are likely:

- to have statements that have slightly nuanced changes of detail, making it hard to tell whether they are right or wrong.
- not to offer clear statements of fact but to infer opinions or judgements and therefore require the higher-order skill of reading between the lines.
- to draw on large sections or pages of text.
- to use in the questions language that is very different from that in the original text.

The following example is constructed from p. 38 of *Foundations*, and is a much less satisfactory way of helping low-aged readers into a challenging text. It has too many weaknesses to be a low-level entry exercise. Firstly, it draws on a large section of text and the diagram. Secondly, it gives statements which are a complex summary of the information on the page – making it essential for the reader to use the high-level literacy skill of reading between the lines.

The vast majority of the world's water supply, suitable for humans, is stored in unusable forms. *True or false?*

In Britain, rivers are a more reliable source of water than lakes. *True or false?*

Water is transferred to large cities using underground distribution systems. *True or false?*

There are more reservoirs in the north of England because this is where there is the greatest demand for water. *True or false?*

Answers: T, F, T, F.

Differentiation that encourages pupils to write independently

So far in this chapter we have looked at DARTs that have encouraged pupils to focus their understanding on small important chunks of text. We have also seen how DARTs can be used to create a structured written response through essentially ready-made writing. By 'ready-made' I mean that pupils select individual words to add to a text (cloze exercise). Or they decide what order to put sentences in (sequencing) or judge whether a statement is right or wrong (true or false exercises). The main body of writing is written and structured by somebody other than them. But the secondary curriculum in many subjects demands that all pupils should write extended open-ended assignments.

Low-aged readers find this task particularly difficult. They often find writing their own sentence hard, let alone turning that into a paragraph or a page. As their learning support teacher, you'll need to find strategies to help them write longer narratives both in class and in withdrawal situations.

Key Stage Three and Key Stage Four subjects across the board make demands for a variety of writing styles. These are the main ones, which we shall look at in detail below:

- writing a discussion
- writing an explanation
- writing to persuade
- writing instructions
- recounting (either a story or non-fiction information)

Writing frames and word prompts

The most effective way of helping struggling readers begin to write in a structured but independent way is to give them writing frames and lists of appropriate word prompts.

Writing a discussion

This is a likely format in English, history, science, religious studies and design technology. In this sort of writing pupils need to present both sides of an argument but end up deciding in favour of one point of view. In its most sophisticated form it is the staple diet of degree courses, but the rudiments can be taught as early as primary school. Here is a simple example to show you how you can lay out a formal writing exercise for your pupils.

Should Britain have the Queen or a President?

Introductionary paragraph

This will outline that this is a piece of writing based on the central subject of whether Britain should have a monarchy or not. Explain the main differences. The Queen is head of Britain because she was born to the job, but a president is elected by the people.

Arguments on each side

Arguments against having the Queen

She is not elected like a President, so nobody really chooses her.

It costs millions of pounds of taxpayers' money to keep all the royal castles running and have all the royal ceremonies etc.

Why should one woman be given a special privilege over all other people, just because she was born into the royal family? etc.

Arguments for having the Queen

The Queen is part of Britain's tradition, history and heritage.

Many people are fond of the Queen, as if she was a part of their own family.

The Queen is famous the world over. Indirectly, she makes money for Britain by bringing tourists into the country.

Concluding paragraph

A summary of the most important arguments for and against having a Queen. This is a chance for the pupils to state their personal position on the argument.

Here is a simple writing frame for discussion writing, which you could use as a pro-forma.

Today we are going to discuss:

The arguments for include points such as:

The arguments against include points such as:

The strongest argument *for* is:

The strongest argument *against* it is:

After looking at both sides of the argument, I think that:

Besides using a basic format writing frame for 'argument', it's also useful to give your pupils important words and phrases that can be used again and again with this kind of writing:

On the one hand . . .

One point of view is that . . .

It could be argued . . .

There is some evidence that . . .

Some people feel that . . .

Useful 'prompt' words include:

consequently . . .   since . . .
therefore . . .   in fact . . .

Writing to explain

All secondary National Curriculum subjects require writing to explain. These lists of useful words will help pupils shape their writing. They are useful lists for you to keep close at hand.

Words for explaining why:

because	therefore
as	since
consequently	as a result

Words for getting ideas in order:

firstly, secondly,	then
finally	afterwards
next	eventually
meanwhile	in addition

Words for giving examples:

such as
for example
suggested by

Words for comparing ideas:

despite this	equally
on the other hand	compared to
whereas	despite this
although	

Words for stressing ideas:

in particular	above all
more important	especially
significantly	

Words for concluding:

in conclusion	in summary
to conclude	to sum up

Writing frames for explanation:

I would like to explain why . . .	Also you can see . . .
There are several reasons for this . . .	A further reason is . . .
The main reason is . . .	To sum up . . .
Another reason is . . .	

Writing to persuade

This is another style of writing that is likely to come up in some shape or form in every subject area of the secondary curriculum. Writing to persuade requires giving your view on something and backing it up with examples. There is a useful bank of words and phrases which you can encourage literacy recovery pupils to delve into in order to help develop their persuasive skills:

It is clear from . . . that . . .	In particular . . .
These facts show . . .	Since . . .

What's more . . .   Clearly . . .
Therefore . . .   Certainly . . .
Above all . . .   Obviously . . .
In fact . . .

Here is a simple 'persuasion' writing formula:

Here is my big point.   Point 2
I can back it up with little points.   Point 3
Point 1   In summary, I think the most important point is . . .

Here is a 'persuasion' writing frame:

I would like to argue that . . .
There are several important reasons for arguing this point of view.
My first reason is . . .
My second reason is . . .
Another reason is . . .
What's more . . .
I think I have shown that . . .

Writing instructions

Another common form of writing is 'procedural'. It takes the reader, step by step, through a process. It's a 'how-to-do-something' type of writing. It begins by stating a purpose and then describing the steps to achieve the goal. This is commonly required writing skill in English, Design Technology and Science at secondary school level. It usually takes the form of Instructions. Here is a procedural writing frame:

This is how you . . .
You will need to . . .
First you . . .
Then you . . .
Next you . . .
After that, you . . .
Finally . . .

Writing to recount

You will probably need to support your pupils with recount writing in several ways. Recount comes in the shape of fictional story telling and in form of non-fictional information dissemination. As a non-fiction skill, recount is essential to most parts of the secondary National Curriculum. Creative writing around story telling remains a much-used technique in Years 7 and 8 of the English Curriculum.

Here are some simple guidelines you could use to help pupils to harness their imagination for writing a short story. Rehearse these questions with the pupils orally before you get them to write anything.

Guideline for a story:

What is the situation at the start of your story?
What will happen to this situation which will change it, in an interesting way?
How does the story develop from the moment you bring in this big change?
How does the story end?

Is there a turning point or sudden twist in your story?
Is there a neat end to your story or are problems left unsolved?

Writing frame for non-fiction:

It began when . . .
This meant that . . .
After that . . .
Then . . .
Also . . .
Finally . . .

There are also useful words and phrases for recount writing which move the action along.

Meanwhile . . .	However . . .	Afterwards . . .
Later . . .	Eventually . . .	I remember . . .
Especially . . .	Although I realise now . . .	First of all, I felt . . .
Strangely . . .	There must be . . .	Perhaps . . .

Further reading

Blum, P. (2001) *Werewolf Eclipse* (Learning Design). Used in the text to model Differentiation in this chapter. From a series of six low aged readers for teenagers based on *The X Files* called The Extraordinary Files. Telephone 020 7093 4051, website *www.learningdesign.biz*

Durran, J. and Stewart, J. (2000) *A Student Handbook for English* (Pearson). This the simplest, most lucid guide to how to write in different styles and for different audiences that I have seen. It's a gem of a book and would be well worth buying for yourself and any students you work with. At the time of writing, the publication was very cheap and good value for money. It's written by two serving heads of English.

Grant, K. (2001) *Supporting Literacy: A Guide for Primary Classroom Assistants* (Routledge/Falmer). This book has some very useful exemplar writing frames in the photocopiable section at the back.

Peer, L. and Reid, G. (eds), *Dyslexia: Successful Inclusion in the Secondary School* (David Fulton in association with the British Dyslexia Association). The book has interesting sections on how dyslexic pupils can be encouraged to make the most of each National Curriculum subject area at secondary school. There are some useful practical tips for each of the subject areas.

Making Reading Easier, Basic Skills Agency pamphlet. This lucid little guide gives practical details about how size, lay-out and presentation of text can make a big difference to its accessibility for low-aged readers. It has many practical hints on how a teacher may decide to differentiate complex text. Available free of charge from Admaill 524, London WC1A 1BR, telephone 0870 600 2400. One useful hint whether you read the whole pamphlet or not is to remember that, like most readers, struggling readers find upper case typing much harder to read than mixed upper and lower case. So LEEDS is much harder than Leeds, CHELSEA is much harder than Chelsea.

Chapter 7

Spelling and reading

Spelling is the toughest single literacy problem to deal with. To spell correctly, your pupil has to be one hundred per cent accurate in their recall of every letter, whereas to read with one hundred per cent accuracy you scan words without needing a photographic recall of each and every letter sequence you see. Spelling is the literacy skill that can trigger off the highest level of emotional frustration and negativity from secondary school students. They have had years of covering up for spelling limitations and many have long since given up trying to improve it. Even pupils with otherwise mature literacy skills often find that their spelling is still an area of weakness.

So approaching the issue of spelling with poor secondary readers is to some extent a controversial issue. For a minority of pupils, it may be best to miss out work on spelling altogether and concentrate on improving their reading skills only. For the majority, working on strategies to improve their spelling will also lead to an increased confidence in their reading accuracy and fluency. Using a variety of spelling strategies helps these poor readers recognize a more extensive **sight vocabulary**, improving their **lexical** reading skills. Other spelling strategies may help them improve their **segmenting** and **blending** skills, so vital to the **sub-lexical** reading route of sounding out individual words. Becoming a better speller can be an important strategy in becoming a better reader.

Spelling: a background

Spelling development in young children

There has been a lot of research on how children learn to spell. Like any complex literacy field, there is a lot of expert argument about exactly what happens and how it happens, but there is a general consensus that learning how to spell goes through defined stages of development.

1   *Early communication.* Young children try to write for the first time. Their writing contains a mixture of actual letters, numerals and made-up symbols. No reader will be able to make real sense of it, although the young writer may be able to explain what they wanted to say.
2   *Semi-phonetic communication.* Children begin to understand that letters link to sounds as they begin to have knowledge of the alphabet and word formation. They may start to write simple words with the right initial letter sounds.
3   *Full phonetics.* The phonology of sound/symbol linkage is now a regular part of children's spelling. They are getting to know simple letter strings and consonant-vowel-consonant words (CVC words). They can see the patterns of certain **onset** and **rime** groups.
4   *Phonetic and other spelling strategies.* Children become less reliant on sound-to-letter mapping. They are beginning to use visual techniques to remember irregular words. They have a strong awareness of accepted letter strings and some generalizations of spelling.
5   *Mature spelling.* Children emerge as independent spellers, with accurate spelling in a large number of words – regular and irregular. They have a basic understanding of the rules and patterns of English and are able to use a variety of visual strategies to recognize words. These

children will probably know the difference between homophones such as 'pear' and 'pair' or homographs such as 'tear' as in crying and 'tear' as in ripping.

The National Literacy Strategy on spelling

The National Literacy Strategy places spelling under 'Word Work' in the *Framework for Teaching* document. It encourages spelling by mapping sounds to letters in very young children. By the time children enter secondary school at Key Stage Three, the NLS sensibly suggests a wider range of strategies, many of which we will look at later in this chapter.

The mystery of the 'good speller'

A lot of controversy and mystery surrounds the art of spelling. Good spellers, like good readers, don't often remember what explicit strategies they used to learn their skill. For many, it's just an unconscious talent they acquired. For the majority, a lot of reading was enough to reinforce their spelling skills. Sometimes they will tell you that they learned to spell by having a lot of spelling tests at school. But when they are asked how they actually learned the spellings for the tests, they can't really remember a particular strategy. Perhaps they knew most of them already and simply wrote them out correctly for the test. It's likely that they combined three particular skills which poor spellers often lack:

- a good visual memory for what they had seen in print while reading
- a secure motor movement memory, so that they remembered automatically how their hand should move across a page to form a word correctly. In situations when they were not sure, they would simply write the word out in a couple of versions and assess which one 'felt right', in terms of movement.
- a good aural memory for the sounds in words and which combinations of letters represent them on each occasion.

Good spellers find that spelling words right comes so naturally to them that they do it intuitively and without conscious effort. Obviously, this will be the situation that many literacy teachers find themselves in. Yet, what poor-spelling pupils need more than anything else are *explicit* strategies for teaching them how to spell better. The intuition and unconscious talent of their teachers won't help them.

Unless you are a learning support teacher who had a lot of difficulties learning to spell yourself, you will need to learn those explicit strategies before you can help others. Without this effort, 'good spellers' are not natural teachers of spelling.

Key intervention strategies for improving spelling

If you take account of suggestions here, you can help most of your weak readers improve their spelling.

- Remember that each of your pupils is an individual with their own particular learning styles. You need to work out exactly what they are finding difficult before you can come up with an effective intervention. Careful diagnosis of spelling problems is vital.
- You'll need to experiment with strategies for getting your pupils to spell better. No one method is right for all pupils. A strategy that one pupil thrives on will be a dead loss to another.
- Build up a spelling intervention around your students' strengths. Use the good points of the way they spell already to move them forward.
- As a good speller, you might know of one particular strategy that helps you when you get stuck. But your strategy may be a real turn-off to the pupil in your charge. You may have to experiment with strategies for remembering how to spell words which are completely alien to your

own personal learning style. Teaching something in a manner which you don't relate to personally is never easy, so you need to stay aware of that problem and consciously compensate for it. There's no point trying to impose your way of learning spellings on a pupil.

- Many of your pupils will hate spelling. You'll need to use a lot of positive reinforcement of the kind we looked at in Chapter 2 to bolster their confidence.
- Try to teach spelling through words that the student needs to use for real writing assignments. Disassociated word lists will never be as effective as words for immediate consumption.
- A new word spelt correctly in a spelling test given to a pupil is a very positive sign. But it should be the beginning of a regular programme of reinforcement in which you return again and again to old lists of words to see whether the pupil can still get them right. To keep on spelling a word correctly means putting it in the long-term memory.
- Learning how to spell better is predominantly the result of weak spellers finding strategies which help them feel more confident about facing up to their own spelling problems, rather than continuing to bury them. It's a process of tackling spelling. If your learner gets that process right, then the number of words they can learn to spell well is unlimited. Eventually, they will be able to take control of the process themselves.

Assessment of spelling difficulties

To diagnose spelling problems effectively, you need to look at several types of pupils' writing. To conduct a spelling error analysis that has validity, this writing needs to be long enough to give you at least twenty-five errors to diagnose a pattern of spelling deficiencies from.

Pick out a piece of independent writing from class done under normal circumstances (no extra help provided) or a piece of independent writing done specially for you, where the pupil is given no extra help or support. In both types of assessment, be aware that pupils may be playing it safe and using only the words which they believe they can spell accurately.

If you want to delve deeper into the spelling patterns of one of your pupils, then you should give them a short dictation.

Dictation

Dictation allows you to decide which words you want the pupils to spell. Try to pick a passage which corresponds closely to what they can read comfortably. Dictation is useful in that it forces pupils to try to spell words in a real writing context. Try to make the dictation passage at least 250 words long.

Lists of words

An alternative or a supplement to a short piece of dictation is to ask a pupil to spell out a list of words. You can supply a list of words for pupils to spell, which allows you to give them specific types of words – sometimes high-frequency irregular words or maybe words which follow a phonetic pattern or have a certain onset and rime. For example 'ought' with 'sought' and 'bought' or 'right' with 'light' and 'fight'. There are many such word lists in the Reason and Boote book and the British Spelling Test series referenced at the end of this chapter.

You can use two other useful techniques to maximize the information you can get from the written assessments.

Observation and participation

Watch pupils

As the pupils attempt to spell in the test you have given them, try to watch how they work, with some of the following questions in mind:

- Can the pupils spell some words straight off? Which ones do they have to think about?
- Can you see them sounding out words under their breath?
- Can you see whether they are actually writing the sounds that they are saying?
- Do they write out versions of the word to see whether it looks right?
- Are they capable of correcting their own mistakes? At once? Or do they go back later in the test? What do their faces tell you: are they worried about making a mistake or utterly unconcerned as they plough on regardless?

Obviously you shouldn't sit next to them and peer over their shoulders while they are writing as that is guaranteed to put them right off. But you could do some detective work from a few feet away, sitting either directly behind them or opposite them as they write.

Talk to pupils

As soon as it's finished and the experience is still fresh in their minds, talk to pupils about the strategies they've used in the spelling test as you are going through the answers with them. This is a series of possible questions you could keep in mind:

- What sort of words do they find hard to spell and which easy?
- Are they ever brave enough to learn how to spell a word on their own?
- How do they set about learning the spelling of a word?
- How good do they think their spelling is?
- Can they work out which words they have spelt wrong?
- What do they do when they cannot spell a word in a lesson? Guess? Use a different word? Leave the word out, or ask a teacher or another pupil for help?
- How personally motivated do they feel in themselves about improving their own spelling?

Analysis of the writing you receive

Much has been written about how to analyse spelling mistakes and how to decide whether the pattern demonstrates a speller with aural (hearing) or visual (sight) weaknesses or motor skill deficiencies (hand co-ordination across the page). I believe that it's very difficult to tell by looking at a spelling mistake whether your pupil has predominantly aural, visual or motor skill weaknesses. I've come across many pupils who seem to have a combination of the three.

What we already know is that most of the low-aged readers you will deal with in secondary school will have weak sound-to-letter mapping skills when decoding text. They will transfer this weakness with a vengeance to spelling words. They may hear the sound but they don't convert it well into strings of letters. Many also have poor visual memories and some overuse visual memory to compensate for their poor phonological skills. The likely scenario from a spelling dictation of a passage or a word list is poor spelling as a result of both visual and phonological errors.

Your challenge is to find strategies that help those pupils learn how to spell more accurately – and through those strategies change their level of self-confidence about being able to spell.

Likely types of error

The three most likely reasons for a pupil making errors are:

- *visual or sequencing errors*: pupils get letters the wrong way round, because of poor visual memory: 'poelpe' for 'people'
- *phonetic problems*: pupils do not know that the sound they are hearing maps to a particular series of letters and may use the wrong ones: 'hart' for 'heart'. But they are often capable of spelling it as it sounds, using a recognisable letter string.

- *hearing errors*: pupils are unable to hear and identify a sound, so it's missed out in their writing of a word: 'natal' for 'natural' or 'folling' for 'following' and 'secesly' for 'scarcely'.

These errors are likely to become more pronounced on longer multisyllable words.

It's also possible that pupils hear a the sound but fail to writing it down because they are unsure of which letters to use (phonetic problems again) or because they hear the sound but have poor visual memory for the way the word looks, even though, in theory, they know which letters map to which sounds. So dividing pupils' spelling problems into neat categories is very difficult.

What to look for

In a spelling error analysis, watch:

- to see whether there are any obvious patterns to the mistakes the pupil makes – without trying to pigeonhole them into a visual or aural weakness box. Watching them spell and asking questions about how they spell helps to make any diagnosis more accurate.
- to see what range of words they are spelling correctly. Knowing their strengths is as important as assessing their weaknesses.
- to examine the contexts in which they make mistakes. Are they more inclined to mistakes in freestyle writing or in single-word passage dictation? Do they spell better or worse in test conditions?
- to compare their spelling difficulties with what we already know about their reading.
- to examine their attitude to their own spelling. Are students picking up on their own spelling errors through checking their own work? Are they capable of it? Can they be bothered?

Here is an example of a simple error analysis grid for spelling:

Intended word	Spelt	Possible analysis
card	kard	Phonetically possible.
stair	stars	Could be mishearing middle of the word or doesn't know how to write the 'ai' sound.
happy	hapi	Rule on 'pp' and 'y' ending. But it's phonetically correct.
thought	fort	Again phonetically correct.
loneliness	lolones	Seems to be finding this multisyllable word hard to hear. Hasn't mapped sounds well. But it's a long word – could be a visual mistake.

Concluding notes

X seems very anxious during the dictation. No attempt to change spellings after he's written them. He doesn't seem to be sounding out words under his breath.

Such a grid allows you flexibility in the way you diagnose a mistake. It works best if you give yourself time to fill it in properly. That might mean at least five minutes at the end of the test, so you can ponder on what you've seen.

Looking at spelling mistakes with the pupil

Try to pick out words that are spelt correctly or nearly right. Comment positively on what the pupil has already achieved.

If some words are spelt phonetically correct so they are easily understandable, even where wrong letter strings are used, point this out and boost their confidence: for example 'jigantick' for 'gigantic' or 'sirface' for 'surface'.

If you can pick out a particular pattern of problems out, then do so. Stress that the pupil may have a particular learning difficulty around this pattern of mistakes. Pupils will often feel better if they understand a clear link between a learning difficulty they have and spelling mistakes they've made. It helps to relieve the frustration they feel about being a weak speller. For example a pupil will probably feel better for knowing that they have an auditory difficulty in hearing all the sounds in a word – particularly letter blends such as 'sc'. This is why they are spelling 'scare' as 'sare.'

Explain to pupils that you will offer them a range of ways to help them improve their spelling, and it will be their choice to pick ones they feel comfortable with.

Types of spelling intervention

Experts say that the following points influence success in the teaching of spelling

- Keep the number of words to be learnt down to no more than four or five a day. In a week, fifteen properly remembered words would be a good result.
- Try to test daily and not weekly.
- Teach words that the students wants to write.
- Base these lists on words that they are spelling wrong in their own work.
- Look carefully at misspellings with the students. Ask them to explain why they selected the spelling they did and whether they can see an alternative for it now.
- Focus particularly on 'hard bits' in words.
- Try to get your student to make links between words they can spell already and words they want to spell – for example, 'caught' is like 'taught'.
- Look at a whole range of multi-sensory strategies to encourage spelling in which seeing, hearing and speaking are used to remember the word.
- Use plenty of praise and positive rewards to motivate the pupils. Learning to spell better should be a process they get really involved in. You need to create a strong sense of purpose and momentum around it.
- Involve the parents if you can, in the frequent short testing regime you'll need to create.

Strategies around aural processing

Significant research around secondary pupils learning how to improve their spelling suggests that it's hard to improve sound-to-letter mapping and phonological awareness by the time pupils are past the age of eleven.

I would recommend the same type of light-touch phonic interventions suggested in Chapter 3. Boggle diagrams get the pupils to focus on the structure of words and experiment with spelling. Quick segmenting or blending exercises around words that a pupil is trying to spell may help to build their phonic awareness for building words.

Visual strategies

Most schools of thought accept that working on older pupils' visual memory is an important strategy for making them better spellers. I am going to focus on strategies that I've seen tried in secondary school settings. Significant numbers of pupils have responded positively to them. They are also strategies that are quick and easy to use, with no cutting up cards, making plastic letters or using plasticine. There is nothing wrong with such resource-based approaches, but the emphasis in this chapter is on interventions that don't require much preparation.

Look, Cover, Write and Check

This is often taught as the one and only way of improving spelling. We are going to explore how it can be expanded.

Look, Cover, Write and Check is a very visual strategy. The pupil looks at the word and tries to visualize it in their mind's eye. The word is covered and the pupil writes it from memory. The word is uncovered and the pupil checks it. If it is incorrect, the pupil starts the process again, keeping on until they get it right.

This is a good structural basis for interventions aimed at strengthening specific aspects of visual memory. To make it more multi-sensory, you can make the process Look, Cover, Write, *Say* and Check.

We will examine other important strategies that you can use during the 'Look' part of the process to make the visual input more powerful. For example you can explore the strategy of getting your pupil to focus on a meaningful chunk of the word. This is sometimes referred to as chunking.

The 'word within the word'

A word itself is the most obviously recognizable chunk of another word. For example:

* *textiles* – word within word: 'Text' or 'tiles'
* *daddy* – word within word: 'add'
* *repeat* – word within word: 'pea' or 'peat'
* *weird* – word within word: 'weir'
* *knowledge* – word within word: 'know' or 'led' or 'ledge'.

There are endless examples in the English language of this happening.

If the pupil can't locate a 'word within a word' association or doesn't find that part of the word difficult to remember, then there may be a significant part of the word that the pupil does accept is vital to remember for spelling purposes. For example:

parents **cha**o**s **spe**c**ific di**arrhoea**

o**cc**as**i**o**n – two cs and one s

ne**cess**ary – one c and two ss

argu**e** is with an e and argument is without an e

As always, what two people pick as significant strings of letters may be very different.

Spelling in syllables

Often pupils find it helpful to break a word down into syllables to see whether there's a part of a word that lends it itself to 'highlighting' and committing to memory. Words can be broken down into their syllables in different ways. For example, 'accommodate' can be *acc-ommo-date* or *ac-com-mod-ate*. The pupil's personal taste will dictate the way they prefer to try and remember the way the word is built. It depends on which parts of that word they find difficult to remember.

Adding to the visual dimension

Once pupils have found parts of the word they need to focus on, one useful strategy to emphasize it is to highlight it:

* by shading or colouring it in.
* by drawing a picture that helps give a distinctive association to the meaning of the word.

Here are some practical examples:

Entrance   EntrAnce

This was the problematic letter for one pupil. Having highlighted it, he saw that the A was rather like looking at the entrance to a tent. He turned the A into a picture of a tent. This little drawing became his way of remembering the vowel sound.

Combining visual strategies with other senses

Some pupils combine the drawing of the pictures with key letters which they label:

anaesthetic

The problem letters to memorize were *a* and *e*. Having coloured them, the pupil drew little pictures, *a* for apple and *e* for egg, and chanted the two key words to herself. So now every time the pupil sees the word 'anaesthetic', the visual and aural association of the egg and apple sketch come to mind.

Neurolinguistic spelling strategies

There are a variety of strategies based on what pupils can see when they shut their eyes and visualize words in their heads. The sheer imaginative variety of these methods will appeal to some of your target group. Anything that entertains or enthuses them is good for the art of spelling better.

The student looks at a word on a page and then looks up to the left-hand corner of the wall, shuts their eyes and forms a mental picture of a pleasant or familiar scene. Then they look down at the page of the book, open their eyes and look carefully at the word they want to learn (up to ten seconds). As they do it, they try to put it into the top left part of their field of vision.

Then the student shuts their eyes and looks up to the left, and tries to see the word again in the midst of their favourite setting. If they can't recall it all on the first showing, they look back at the word on the page and then back into the special place in the top left-hand corner of the room.

Some variations on this theme are:

- eyes open or eyes shut, when putting the word in the top left-hand corner of the room
- putting the word into their favourite colour, if this helps them remember it
- putting certain difficult letter formations in the word in a different colour or in bigger letters to make them stand out
- tracing the letters in the air or on their arm.

Mnemonics

Mnemonics are a combination of a visual and an aural strategy. The student comes up with a rhyme or phrase to help them remember a whole word or the tricky part of a word. Here are some common variations.

Short mnemonics

These are useful for bits of words or certain letter combinations:

Dessert

The double *ss* distinguishes this word 'dessert' from a sandy 'desert'. One pupil remembers the *ss* as 'strawberry sundae' and another as 'two sugars'. Both pupils' words associate the *ss* with 'sweetness', which is entirely in keeping with the meaning of 'dessert'.

separat**e**

The pupil remembers the last vowel sound in this adjective with a little rhyme: 'There's a rat in separate.'

kitc**hen**

is remembered with another little rhyme: 'Eat a hen in the kitchen.'

business

One student remembers this tricky word with 'There's a bus in business.'

Mnemonics based on word linkage

Stati**on**ery is to **en**velope.

This time the speller has distinguished between an object which is standing still (stationary) and the office products (stationery) by making a word association with one of the main stationery products – the envelope.

Mnemonics based on acrostics

In acrostics the letters of a word are used as initial letters of words in a made-up sentence:

because

big **e**lephants **c**an't **a**lways **u**se **s**mall **e**xits.

Other spelling strategies

Sounding it out and saying it wrong

Many irregular words in English don't look as they sound. A good strategy for some pupils is to ask them to sound them out phonetically, from the way they look – saying the word the wrong way, to help spell it the right way. This kind of exaggeration is sometimes called *spellspeaking*. Here are some obvious examples:

Wednesday

Say with the *Wed* and the *nes* clearly audible.

i**s**land

An island is what it says, 'is land', so say it like that, to help you with the irregular spelling.

su**b**tle

You can say this incorrectly, with the stress on the *sub*, to remind you of its irregular spelling.

chaos

This is what it says. Say the *ch* like the *ch* in 'church' or 'chance' to help the pupil remember the irregular spelling.

```
tomb = Tom – b
```

Say it phonetically, even though it spells something else which phonetically would be represented *toomber*.

Motor skill memory

Another good way for many spellers to check their memory of words is a physical process, rewriting them again to see if the movement across the page feels right.

Obviously it's often helpful to compare two versions of the same word on the page, visually. But it's the automatic act of handwriting a word that can help some pupils: it feels as though it is spelled correctly.

A word bank

Whichever spelling strategies suit your literacy recovery pupils, they will need to amass a list of the words they are trying to learn.

Constant repetition of spelling is vital. Old word lists need constant revisiting over long periods of time. You can help your pupils if you encourage them not only to record the words and the dates they learnt them but also to make a note of their strategy for learning the word. For example, mnemonic used, word within word highlighted etc.

Spelling games

Don't forget Scrabble and Word Bingo. Both make learning spellings *entertaining* and are therefore a vital strategy for disenchanted secondary pupils.

Barriers to successful spelling intervention

The kind of interventions we have looked at are best done every day, for five minutes. In some schools this is possible but in many the complexities of timetabling and teacher/pupils commitments do not allow meetings of more than once a week, twice if you are lucky.

Involving parents in helping with spelling strategies is also best done when the communication can be made daily rather than weekly. In a busy secondary school this is usually impossible.

Spelling interventions that take place only once a week are difficult to organize effectively. Pupils forget the words they are supposed to be learning or take them home and lose them. Parents forget to look at them. A teacher forgets the words they've set over a seven-day period. It's hard to construct a routine. The vital sense of purpose and momentum that a successful spelling intervention needs doesn't materialize.

Spelling interventions can swallow up large parts of a literacy recovery session because of their highly personal one-to-one nature. It's always best to give pupils their own words to learn and spend individual time with them, selecting a successful strategy for remembering them. It's likely that you will give each pupil an individual spelling test for the words they are supposed to have mastered. If you have a group of six pupils, it starts getting hard to give them so much personal attention without eating into time for reading recovery itself. If you see them once a week only, the problem gets very acute.

Spelling tests on a particular list of five words need to be revisited at least every month and returned to over a year. Pupils with memory problems will forget what they've learnt. The ever-growing backlist needs constant reinforcement.

Ways around these problems

Look carefully at how you can obtain flexible timetabling arrangements for yourself. You need short interventions if possible. Fifteen minutes, four times a week, are more effective than sixty minutes once a week. This is true for all types of literacy recovery work – especially spelling.

Send notes home via the pupil to the parents. Phone them or meet them face-to-face at the beginning of the year to explain their role in helping their son or daughter with your spelling intervention. It would be useful if you could go through some of the spelling strategies that you will be showing the pupils, or at least to give the parents a summary sheet illustrating them.

See whether you can work out ways in which the parent can give emotional support for the process. Refer back to Chapter 2 about linking rewards to small steps of progress.

Remember that many of the pupils you are seeing are not only poor spellers, they also find it hard to organize themselves. Encourage parents to keep their own running record of the lists of spellings being learned. Then if the pupil loses their spelling word bank, the situation can be salvaged.

Reinforce, revisit, reinforce. For a spelling strategy to be successful you need to keep on going back over words pupils learnt five weeks ago or even eight months ago. In revisiting particular words you also revisit the strategies and processes that either have or haven't worked for the pupils with that word. When a word needs learning a second or third time, you might encourage a pupil to try a new spelling strategy on it. Maybe the pupil has explored other strategies successfully since learning the word first time.

Keep pupils' spelling word banks close to hand. When you are reading, you may be able to find a way of linking a new word they need to spell with a word family, rule or spelling pattern they're already familiar with.

In-class support: specific ways to intervene in supporting spelling

If the mainstream class teacher has already highlighted spelling errors in written work, encourage the pupils to use them as words for their word bank and personal spelling strategy.

Take a group of pupils aside to work on individualized spelling strategies, while the mainstream teacher does something else with the rest of the class.

In-class strategies involving checking

Ask a pupil to reread a part of their work. Whether it's a page, paragraph or just a sentence depends on the learning difficulties of the individual. Instruct the pupil to look for their own mistakes and underline any words that they suspect that they have made a spelling mistake on.

Depending on the pupil and the volume of mistakes they have made, you might ask the pupil to attempt self-correction of the words they've underlined. How much you ask the pupil to do will inevitably depend on the golden rule – not to demoralize and overwhelm them with feelings of hopelessness and negativity. If there are many mistakes and the pupil seems to notice and underline only a few of them, it's probably best to let the others go and concentrate on a few simple steps forward with the self-selected words.

It can be a useful strategy to ask pupils to work in pairs and check each other's work. They may miss some mistakes but they can compare their ways of learning words. This kind of collaboration can bring some enjoyment into working on spelling.

Summary of key points

Spelling is the most finely balanced and complex literacy skill to make significant progress on. Secondary pupils with reading and writing difficulties usually find this the most challenging area to improve on. But improving a poor reader's spelling is likely to improve their reading at the same time.

The most crucial strategy for spelling better is the personal desire to succeed at it and conquer the problem. Building up a positive emotional commitment to improving spelling is the one essential strategy. Without it, no other spelling technique can work. If the pupil remains half-hearted in their commitment to improve spelling, you would be better to concentrate on other aspects of their literacy.

Pupils may not settle on just one personal spelling strategy and use it all the time. Many adopt a whole range of spelling strategies in an eclectic way – mnemonics for one word, chunking for another and neuro-linguistic for a third. You must introduce them to as many as you can.

For spelling interventions to be effective, it's much better to do them a little and often. Ten minutes of one-to-one time on how to improve spelling is worth more than two hours of whole-class time on 'general approaches'.

Further reading and useful resources

Vincent, D. and Crumpler, M. (1997) *British Spelling Test Series* (NFER–Nelson). Lots of different types of spelling tests and useful word lists.

Reason, R. and Boote, R. (1994) *Helping Children with Reading and Spelling: A Special Needs Manual* (Routledge). Some useful strategies on spelling and some excellent word lists to use for spelling tests.

Millar, R. and Klein, C. (1990) *Making Sense of Spelling: A Guide to Teaching and Leaning on How to Spell* (SENJIT, Institute of Education). An excellent little book that goes through similar information to this chapter. It has some interesting examples of pupils making spelling mistakes, which you could use to make your own diagnosis of spelling problems. In all her publications, Cynthia Klein stresses the importance of finding a personal approach towards improving spelling.

Classroom Resources Ltd is a small company with some good literacy recovery materials around spelling. Their packs are quite expensive but photocopiable. The *Spelling Handbook* is complemented by other useful titles *Mnemonics*, *High Frequency* and *Time Words* packs. Classroom Resources Ltd is based at PO Box 1489, Bristol BS99 3QJ.

Chapter 8

Using Information Technology

There are many useful practical applications for computers in helping pupils to improve their overall literacy skills.

- Word processing packages such as Microsoft Word can be used by both teacher and pupils to great effect – in particular, to write user-friendly text for pupils to read aloud to their support worker. These home-made texts are often much more effective than a commercially produced reading book or structured reading scheme (see pp. 45–48 for more details).
- There is software to help pupils structure their writing by creating writing scaffolds for them.
- There are useful software applications to help with spelling.
- There are integrated learning packages such as *Successmaker* that support pupils with both literacy and numeracy.

This chapter concentrates on IT applications which learning support teachers will find it easiest to gain access to.

Pupils using word processors

Microsoft Word is the most common word processing program in use in secondary schools. It can be used simply and effectively to help support pupils with both their reading and writing.

The planning stage

When pupils are deciding what they want to write, a word processor can be used to store phrases or sentences that would be helpful in that writing process. These can be entered by the teacher and pupil 'brainstorming' them, or by the teacher preparing key words or phrases in advance. What the teacher and pupil compose together is often excellent textual material for the pupil to read aloud.

The composition stage

When a pupil gets down to the business of writing, the word processor is particularly unthreatening because ideas can be added, changed or rubbed out without creating a log of demoralizing crossing out and mess.

If you turn the spelling and grammar green and red wavy lines off (*Tools > Options > Spelling and Grammar*), pupils avoid being distracted from what they're writing.

One of the biggest barriers to improving writing is removed – the fear of the risk of failure. At this composition stage, nothing has to stay on screen and anything can be put on screen. The flexibility of the liquid crystal display gives the hesitant student a lot of power.

The checking and correction stage

It's much easier to use a word processor than handwriting to edit out mistakes and change the choice of words. Usually this is done more accurately with a draft printout than on the screen.

Beware of using the 'Spell checker'. It can get a pupil with low literacy skills into all kinds of problems – for example by offering an alternative choice of word which is totally unsuitable.

The publishing stage

This is the 'finished product'. It's at this stage that the word processor really comes into its own.

The printed and finished product can be presented in a very ego-boosting way, using the huge variety of styles, fonts and colours available. A piece of finished work can be stuck inside an exercise book or mounted on a wall. But it can also be posted on a web page, where it could attract a much wider audience. Again, this is a big self-esteem-enhancing exercise, which is always such an important part of any successful literacy recovery work. The pupil can read the finished product aloud again and again, to increase their overall level of confidence and fluency.

Teachers using word processors

Teachers can also use Word to help the pupils. We have seen how you can prepare sentences or phrases for a pupil to incorporate into a piece of structured reading or writing. But you can also prepare templates as ready-made writing frames.

Templates have many advantages:

- They are quick to prepare.
- They are easy to store.
- They can be used again and again for different pupils.

If you look back to the writing frames of Chapter 6, you can see examples of teaching resources that scaffold the writing process in a number of different ways. These kinds of writing frames would make excellent templates on a computer.

Using a laptop word processor to support in-class differentiation

If you are a support teacher doing a lot of in-class support, you can use a laptop to produce many practical resources for the classroom. It takes only a short time to word process the kinds of DARTs we looked at in Chapter 6. With the mainstream class teacher's support you could take ten minutes in the lesson to produce an exercise, print it quickly and photocopy enough copies for it to be incorporated as an activity into the second half of the lesson. This is an excellent way to support the kind of on-the-spot differentiation in the classroom we looked at in Chapter 6. The work you do can be fine-tuned to produce resources for a pupil or groups of pupils with very specific reading and writing difficulties.

Using a word processor with pupils

Dos:

- Plan the writing with the pupil.
- Write a first draft directly on the screen, with the pupil.
- Turn off the grammar and spell check warnings as they inhibit creativity.
- Use font sizes of at least 14 points so that pupils can see clearly what they are reading or writing.
- Do any final editing on a printed copy and not the screen.

Don'ts:

- Worry about spelling mistakes in the first draft.
- Let pupils use spell checkers without your supervision.
- Let pupils use fancy fonts that they will find hard to read.
- Allow the pupils to get sucked into the technical functions of the software rather than the creative process of writing their work and reading it back.

Other software applications

Word grids

Clicker is produced by Crick Software Ltd – telephone 01604 671691, website http://www. cricksoft.com. It allows you to create your own customized cloze exercises like the ones that were demonstrated in Chapter 6. The program provides you with partial or complete sentences to support the writing process.

Spelling programmes

Wordshark is produced by White Space – telephone 0208 748 5927. You can decide how words are grouped and you can add your own customized word lists. The program can keep a record of the pupil's scores and it will print lists of words for the pupils to go away and relearn. It has a variety of games and strategies that encourage successful spelling.

Starspell is software available from Fisher-Marriott – telephone 01394 387 050. It uses the Look, Cover, Write and Check approach to spelling. Words are put in families or subject groups but you can add your own lists if you want to. It keeps a record of pupils' progress and can print out reinforcement word lists for pupils to learn.

Integrated learning systems

Successmaker, produced by Research Machines (telephone 0870 908 6700), is currently the market leader, and the system that many secondary schools have invested heavily in.

This is a numeracy and literacy programme of many levels of difficulty, and pupils are supposed to progress through the levels. They are told by a voice-activated computer whether they are getting the answers correct or incorrect. The program works on the principle that, if they get the answer wrong, pupils will learn from their mistake and get the answer right next time. The *Successmaker* program gives them a printed update how they are scoring. Having seen *Successmaker* in operation in several secondary schools, I can make the following observations.

Good points:

- Many pupils like using it. They are entertained by the process of trying to climb the levels.
- They often concentrate well on it and climb significant numbers of levels.
- They find themselves involved in some useful reading as they set about their tasks.

Points for concern:

- Pupils wear headphones, and learning by using *Successmaker* becomes a solitary and isolating experience. The only interaction is with the computerized voice.
- Pupils have a tendency to pitch themselves in at a level which is too easy for them.
- There's no guarantee that they are learning new skills as they progress up the levels. What they may be learning is the techniques of tricking their way to the right answers.
- The system is very expensive to buy and set up. Could the money be put to better uses?
- It needs additional part- or full-time staffing to maintain the machines, the pupils' progress records and the pupils themselves. Is this the best way to spend such valuable money?

Practical recommendations for integrated learning systems

It's best to use an Integrated Learning System such as *Successmaker* as a part of, not the whole of, a literacy intervention. So pupils should move on to the machines only for fifteen minutes rather than spend a whole lesson on them.

The more a member of staff such as yourself interacts with the pupil as they use the program, the better the chances they'll really learn something. Try to read text with them, rather than let them get completely isolated on headphones for long periods of time.

Conclusions

Good points:

- IT provides some variety. Many pupils like to get involved in it, and the positive feeling it gives them stimulates their learning.
- The simplest IT packages that you know how to use properly yourself are often the best. Microsoft Word, the universal word processing package, is very handy in building up structured reading and writing activities.
- Word is also very useful when employed to produce on-the-spot differentiation during in-class support in mainstream lessons.
- The spelling and word-grid programs can fulfil a valuable function, providing you are comfortable operating them.

 ## Further reading

Dyslexia and I.T. information sheet. Available from http://www.becta.org.uk/technology/infosheets/htoml/dyslexia.html.

Keates, A. (2000) *Dyslexia and Information and Communication Technology: A Guide for Teachers and Parents* (David Fulton).

Conclusion

This book has set out to give a comprehensive introduction to the ways in which you can assess older pupils with poor reading skills and put together programmes to help them improve. It has been written at a time when the extension of the National Literacy Strategy into secondary schools has encouraged more opportunities for learning support teachers to work with small groups of low-aged readers in a structured and regular way in-class or by withdrawal group, through the guided reading initiative in the middle section of an English lesson.

The advice within these pages is only an introduction to what is a complex field. You may want to read more deeply in each of the subjects to which I've given you an overview by reading other books on the reading list at the end of each chapter. If you don't have the time to do this at the moment, I hope that this book has provided you with a range of practical strategies to try out. The strategies I have suggested acknowledge that being a learning support teacher working on reading skills is a challenging job in a secondary school – firstly as a result of pupils having had considerable time to develop negative attitudes towards their own reading, and secondly because not all mainstream subject teachers have the experience they need to work on easing the literacy difficulties of demoralized pupils.

The young people you work with will have their own unique sets of strengths and weaknesses, and a principal feature of your role will be finding a way of getting alongside them emotionally. Ultimately, no intervention can be successful if you are unable to form a positive rapport and bond of trust with those young people. The emotional angle on teaching and learning is as important as any single specialist literacy strategy you attempt to introduce.

Above all else, never forget to try to make learning fun again for your students. There's no point in getting hung up on any one ideology of literacy intervention, but instead mix and match, 'beg, steal and borrow'. The National Literacy Strategy progress units, corrective phonics programmes, spelling software, cloze exercises, reading cues and reward stamps all have their place, if they motivate your pupils. Be as flexible and inventive as you can in striving to reignite a positive state of mind about ' improving reading' in the pupils and teachers that you work with.

Glossary

Blends, blending To read a word by joining together the various sounds represented by the letter combinations. For example *pot/at/o* needs to be moulded together to make the sound of the full word.

Context (reading) Using the meaning and sentence structure to understand the text.

Decoding text Reading words out, the process of sounding them out and pronouncing them correctly, either as a silent narrative or read aloud.

Kinaesthetic Using a sense of feeling or touch to help the learning process.

Lexical A technique for reading. The accomplished reader has the capacity to read whole words by instant recognition. This ability to recognize and read a whole word while simultaneously understanding its meaning is often called the whole-word or lexical route to reading.

Onset The consonant (or consonant cluster) at the beginning of a one-syllable word. For example in the word 'step' the onset is *st*.

Overlearning The teaching strategy of reinforcing a learning objective by repeating it many times with the pupil. This strategy is particularly important with pupils who have a lack of confidence owing to a history of learning difficulty.

Phonic, phonics A system of representing certain sounds by the letters of the alphabet. In this book, phonics is often taken to mean a structured programme of trying to teach this system.

Rime The part of a one-syllable word that follows the onset, consisting of a vowel and rest of the word. For example in the word 'step' the rime is *ep*.

Segments, segmenting Sometimes a reader breaks down an unfamiliar word into its sounds by splitting it up. This is called segmenting. For example the word 'potato' can be broken down into *pot/at/o*.

Sight vocabulary A reader's instantaneous recognition of whole words that allows them both to read and to understand them.

Sub-lexical A technique for reading. Sometimes a reader can't or doesn't want to read a word as a whole. Using the sub-lexical way of reading, they can break a word down into its constituent parts before putting it back together again. This is the segmenting or blending process described in this glossary and is the key to all phonics-based teaching methods.

Index